Model Essays for IB and A Level Economics

MACROECONOMICS Volume 1

Kelvin Hong

Ang Jun Yang

First Printing: 2020

ISBN : 9789811450532

Edventures Pte Ltd

Singapore

www.TheEconomicsTutor.com

Acknowledgments

This work would not have been possible without the help of Jade Chan who helped in drafting and editing the work.

PREFACE

This book answers 20 key examination questions across the entire Macroeconomics syllabus and was created to provide students with the ability to excel in their examinations.

Very often, students are unable to provide step-by-step explanations and relevant evaluation points, which are essential to scoring in examinations.

By studying through the model essays provided in this book, students will also be able to better understand the various economic concepts covered in the Microeconomics syllabus. The powerful diagrammatic analyses provided will also train students to illustrate economic concepts logically, and enable them to use such diagrams for analyses in a more effective and concise manner.

The questions are mostly obtained from past IB examination papers. However, they are also very applicable to the A Level examinations.

We hope students will now see great hope in scoring very well for their essay papers.

Kelvin Hong & Ang Jun Yang

CONTENTS

1. Explain the effect of a rise in savings and a fall in investment on the circular flow of income of an economy. (10)

<u>Introduction</u>

1. The circular flow of income depicts how money as well as goods and services flow through the economy between households and firms. In the economy, income circulates between households and firms endlessly, thereby forming a 'circular flow'.

2. An open economy is most realistically depicted using a five sector circular flow income model, which accounts for the existence of three other economic agents, namely the government, foreign markets, and banks. These three agents are responsible for outflows and inflows of income to the circular flow.

3. In this economy, individuals from households form the labour force that enables businesses to produce goods and services. Individuals earn factor income (Y) from businesses in exchange for their labour. That income is spent on the goods and services produced by businesses, which is termed domestic consumption (Cd).

4. Withdrawals (W) refer to income not spent on domestically produced goods and services and are outflows of national income away from the circular flow. This comprises of savings (S) which are put in banks, taxes (T) which are paid to the government, and import expenditure (M) to foreign markets.

5. Injections (J), on the other hand, refer to spending on domestically produced goods and services other than by domestic households and constitute inflows of income into the circular flow model. This comprises of investment (I) by banks, government spending (G) by the government, and export expenditure (X) by foreigners.

6. When the sum of all withdrawals equal to the sum of all injections (W=J), the circular flow of income will remain the same size and the national income (NY) is at equilibrium.

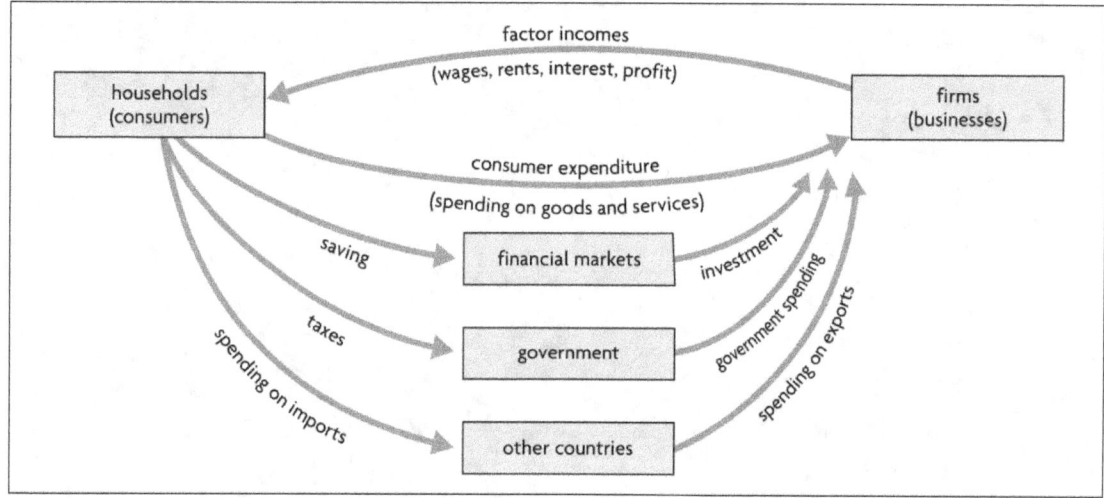

Explanation of effects

1. For example, during the 2008 Great Recession, both households and business confidence levels plummeted over the pessimistic outlook of the economy.

2. As consumers started to panic about a recession, and feared losing their jobs, they began to reduce their C_d and increase their S so as to have enough money to spend on necessities in future should job losses occur. Firms expected lower rates of return on investment projects and fewer profitable investments, translating to a fall in I.

3. The rise in S constitutes an increase in the W from the circular flow, whereas the fall in I constitutes a decrease in the J into the circular flow. This causes $J<W$, ceteris paribus.

4. As C_d and I have fallen, there would be an unplanned increase in inventories, prompting firms to produce less and demand fewer factor inputs from households, resulting in lesser factor income (Y) earned by households.

5. Since households earn less income, they would now be able to consume fewer domestically produced goods and services, which causes another round of a fall in C_d and hence decrease in production and factor incomes. Thus, via the reverse multiplier process, national income (NY) will fall more than proportionately to the initial fall in spending.

6. As incomes fall, households also have less to save in banks, less taxable income, and less to buy foreign goods. This causes S, T and M, and therefore W, to fall as well.

7. The size of the circular flow continues to shrink, until the point where W have decreased sufficiently, to allow for $J=W$ once again. At this stage, the circular flow of income would stabilise and a new NY equilibrium is achieved albeit at a lower level.

8. This analysis assumes that there are no other changes affecting injections or withdrawals. In the real world, the magnitude of injections and withdrawals are constantly changing due to many variable factors, and hence it would be hard for the circular flow of income to ever cease changing in size.

2. Explain the difficulties involved in measuring the rate of inflation. (10)

Introduction

1. Inflation is a sustained increase in the general price level (GPL) of an economy over time.

2. This can be measured by the percentage change in the consumer price index (CPI) over a given time period.

3. The CPI is an index that quantifies the prices of a basket of goods and services that is representative of that consumed by the average household, relative to prices in a given base year.

4. Some goods included in the CPI include food, housing and transportation.

5. Each good is weighted to reflect the relative proportion of income spent by the average household on that good (relative to others in the basket).

Difficulty 1: Basket is not representative

1. The basket of goods and services reflected in the CPI is merely an average. As such, it does not truly reflect the consumption patterns of the high-income and low-income groups.

2. For example, high-income groups are likely to spend more than the average proportion of income on luxury, non-essential items like expensive clothing and gourmet food. Consequently, should prices of these goods increase, it would not accurately capture the increase in cost of living to high-income households, as these goods typically have a smaller weightage in the CPI than what high-income households truly spend on them.

3. The converse holds true for low-income households – they are likely to spend less than the average proportion of income on luxury items, and more than average on necessity items like food and transport. A rise in clothing prices would not translate to a significant increase in their cost of living, as opposed to a rise a food prices; however, these weightages would not be so accurately reflected in the CPI. Thus, should necessities increase in price, an inflation rate of 3% as indicated by the CPI may in fact grossly underestimate the actual inflation rates that the lower-income face.

Difficulty 2: Changes in consumption patterns

1. As the demand for various goods changes over time, so does the proportion of income spent on these goods.

2. For example, in Japan, more households/consumers have been acquiring smartphones in recent years. In 2013, only 24.7% of consumers owned at least one smartphone; this figure increased to 50.1% in 2017. Consequently, the average Japanese consumer now spends a higher proportion of their income on smartphones (and high-end consumer electronics) in 2017 as compared to 2013.

3. Should the weightage of consumer electronics within Japan's CPI not be updated to reflect this changed consumption pattern, this would then render the calculated inflation rate inaccurate.

4. The need to consistently keep up with changing consumption patterns poses a difficulty in measuring inflation rate.

Difficulty 3: Changes in quality of goods

1. As a quantitative measurement, CPI does not take into account the quality of goods.

2. For example, in the US, the establishment of the National Strategy for Quality Improvement in Healthcare in March 2011 sought to improve the quality of healthcare service. Improved patient safety measures in hospitals reduced hospital-acquired infections by 17%, resulting in around 50000 fewer patient deaths.

3. The average consumer of healthcare now receives a higher quality service, which may consequently come at a higher price.

4. The CPI metric alone only takes into account the higher price of healthcare without accounting for the improvement in quality, which may be sufficient to justify the increased prices.

5. This makes measuring inflation rate inaccurate.

Conclusion

1. Therefore, it is evident that establishing an accurate measure of the rate of inflation is fraught with difficulties.

3. Distinguish between structural and demand-deficient unemployment. (10)

Introduction

1. Unemployment refers to the number of individuals who are of working age, are able to work but are without work and are actively seeking a job.

2. Unemployment in an economy comprises the Natural Rate of Unemployment, which refers to any unemployment present when an economy is producing at its full-employment output level, as well as demand-deficient unemployment, which is unemployment resulting from a lack of Aggregate Demand (AD).

Differences between the 2 types of unemployment

1. Structural unemployment occurs as a result of mismatches between the skillsets possessed by workers, and those demanded by firms. This mismatch can arise due to changes in demand for particular types of labour skills, changes in the geographical location of industries, or labour market rigidities.

2. For example, in the past decade, the textile industry in Naoussa, Greece suffered as cheaper Chinese textiles began to flood the market. This resulted in many Greek textile firms going out of business, resulting in the loss of tens of thousands of jobs. These textile workers, who were highly specialised in the production of textiles, were subsequently unable to find a job as the textile industry in Greece began to shrink, and there was no longer strong demand for textile workers.

3. Referring to the diagram below, L1 - L2 number of textile workers would be retrenched. Lacking in the skills needed to work in other sectors, these retrenched workers became structurally unemployed. For example, even though there is an increase in demand for scientists, they are unable to take up the job vacancies in scientific R&D.

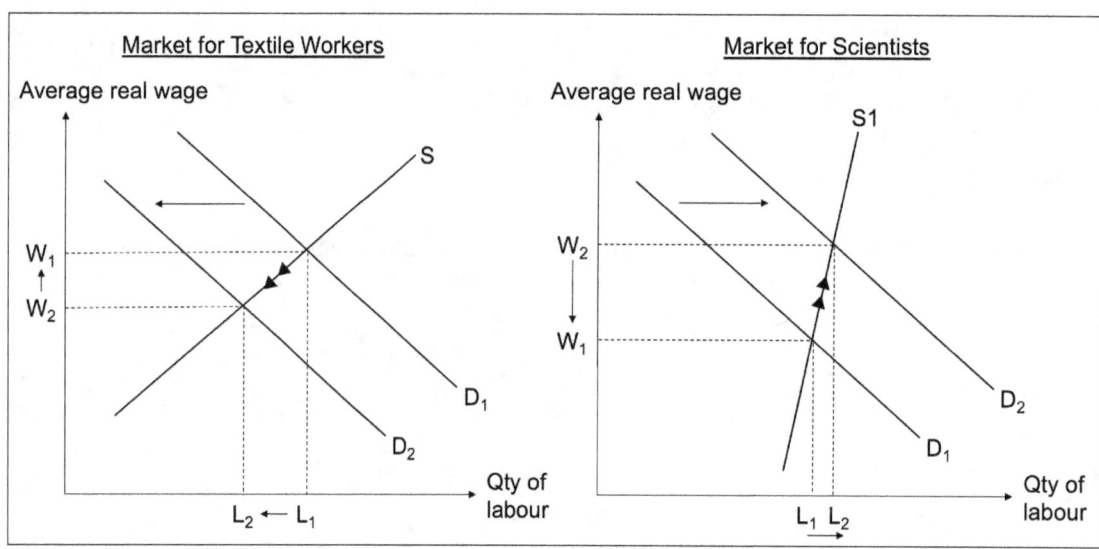

4. On the other hand, demand-deficient unemployment occurs when AD is low and thus the real output of the economy is below full-employment output level. When this happens, firms require less labour, leading to layoffs as they begin to fire workers. Referring to the diagram below, as AD reduces from AD_1 to AD_2, real GDP decreases from Y_1 to Y_2 and hence, AD for labour decreases from AD_{L1} to AD_{L2}. At the prevailing wage W_1, there are more workers willing and able to work than there are job vacancies.

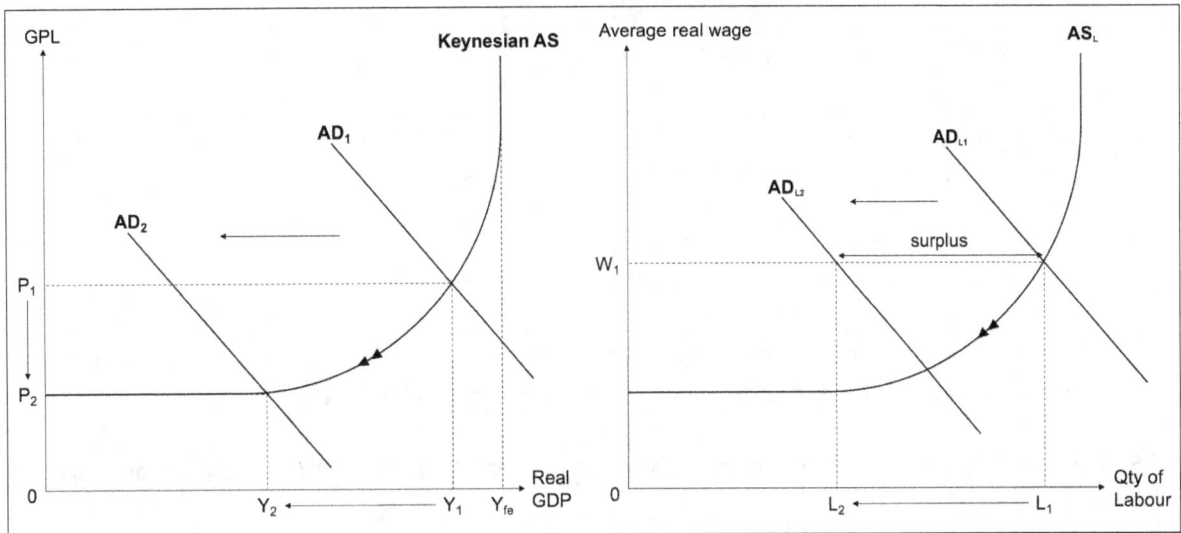

5. For example, during the 2009 recession in the US, a pessimistic business outlook caused falling consumer and investment expenditures, that led to a decreasing AD. During this period, as firms cut back on their production activities, many workers were retrenched, with an estimated 744,000 jobs lost per month in the US. This is a prime example of demand-deficient unemployment.

6. Structural unemployment is an unavoidable issue in the economy that exists even when the economy is performing at full-employment output level. On the other hand, demand-deficient unemployment only exists when the economy is performing below full-employment output level, due to a weak AD.

7. Additionally, structural unemployment implies an issue with the supply-side of the economy, namely that workers are facing a skills mismatch and lack the expertise needed to secure a job. Conversely, demand-deficient unemployment connotes that the demand-side of the economy is deficient in its performance, leading to layoffs as production falls.

4. Explain how business spending on research and development and government expenditure on infrastructure might shift the long-run aggregate supply curve. (10)

<u>Introduction</u>

1. The LRAS curve is vertical at the full employment output level, Y_{fe}.

2. Full employment level of output refers to the maximum output that an economy is capable of producing, assuming full and efficient employment of resources.

3. In the LR, the output that all firms in the economy are willing and able to produce and supply is constant at Y_{fe} regardless of the general price level.

4. The LRAS curve might shift due to the following reasons: a change in the quantity of FOPs, a change in the quality of FOPs or a change in technology.

5. A shift in the LRAS curve would correspond to a change in the country's full employment output.

<u>Business spending on Research and Development (R&D)</u>

1. R&D is the fundamental activity behind the development of new technologies.

2. Firms can undertake R&D in order to achieve process innovation to reduce costs of production.

3. Over the long term, advancement in technology seeks to improve the quality of capital and enhance labour productivity, enabling the same amount of resources to be more productive, i.e. capable of producing a higher level of output. For instance, advancement in technology led to the development of smartphones which promotes increased connectivity and mobility, allowing workers to work 'anytime, anywhere'. Other innovations include the 3D-printers, which has the added capability to produce virtually an unlimited range of functional tools (capital goods) in a short timeframe.

4. Diagrammatically, this is represented as a rightward shift of the LRAS curve from LRAS to LRAS' – at each and every price level P the level of potential output the economy is capable of producing increased from Y_{fe} to Y_{fe}'.

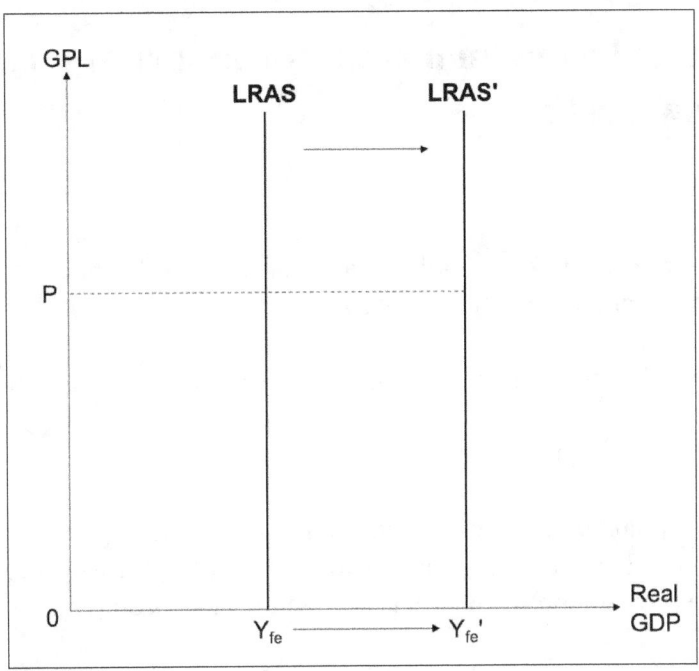

Government expenditure on infrastructure

1. Infrastructure is defined as large scale public systems, such as power supply, telecommunications, and transportation networks, which are usually supplied by the government and are necessary for economic activity.

2. Such infrastructure not only adds to the capital stock of the economy but also promotes productivity.

3. For instance, the Singapore government is currently spending billions in enhancing the country's transportation system, including expansion of the mass transport railway (MRT) network and highways.

4. Good and well-connected roads, railways and other transport systems save time and effort in transporting goods and services, allowing more output to be transported and per-unit costs to be lowered.

5. The availability of effective telecommunications permits faster and easier communications, enabling economic activities to be carried out more efficiently.

6. More and better infrastructure improves labour mobility and thus productive efficiency as well.

7. All these contribute to increasing the full employment level of output, shifting the LRAS curve outwards over the long term – at each and every price level P the maximum level of output the economy is capable of producing increased from Y_{fe} to Y_{fe}'.

5. Explain how labour market reforms may be used to promote economic growth. (10)

Introduction

1. Labour market reforms refer, broadly, to a set of policies designed to increase competition and reduce intervention in the labour market.

2. Labour market reforms are a part of market-oriented supply-side policies.

Examples of Labour Market Reforms

1. One example of labour market reforms involves abolishing or lowering the minimum wage. This would have the effect of lowering the wages for low-skilled workers, thereby decreasing the cost of labour, and hence the unit cost of production of firms.

2. Another example involves weakening the power of trade unions. Margaret Thatcher, the Prime Minister of the UK in the 1980s, was famous for weakening the power of trade unions, making it harder for unions to strike or to bargain for higher wages. As a result, wages were more subject to market forces of demand and supply, and this allowed labour costs to fall.

3. Another instance of labour market reforms can also include reducing unemployment benefits. Recently in the UK, the government announced its decision to reduce unemployment benefits provided to the ill and disabled through the Employment and Support Allowance (ESA) scheme, from £102.15 to £73.10 per week. This would help to prevent a 'crutch mentality' from developing, and would encourage those who are unemployed to seek a job.

Explanation and Diagrams

1. These reforms are designed to reduce the cost of labour, as well as to increase the quantity of labour employed.

2. Reductions in the cost of labour would allow for the unit cost of production of goods and services to decrease. This would incentivise firms to increase their output in the short-run, leading to an increase in the Short-Run Aggregate Supply from $SRAS_1$ to $SRAS_2$.

3. On the other hand, as more people actively seek employment, this increases the quantity of labour, a factor of production (FOP). As a result, this increases the full-employment level of output of the economy, allowing for the Long-Run Aggregate Supply to increase from $LRAS_1$ to $LRAS_2$ as shown in the diagram on the next page.

4. Consequently, the increase in AS causes the real output of the economy to increase from Y_1 to Y_2, leading to EG.

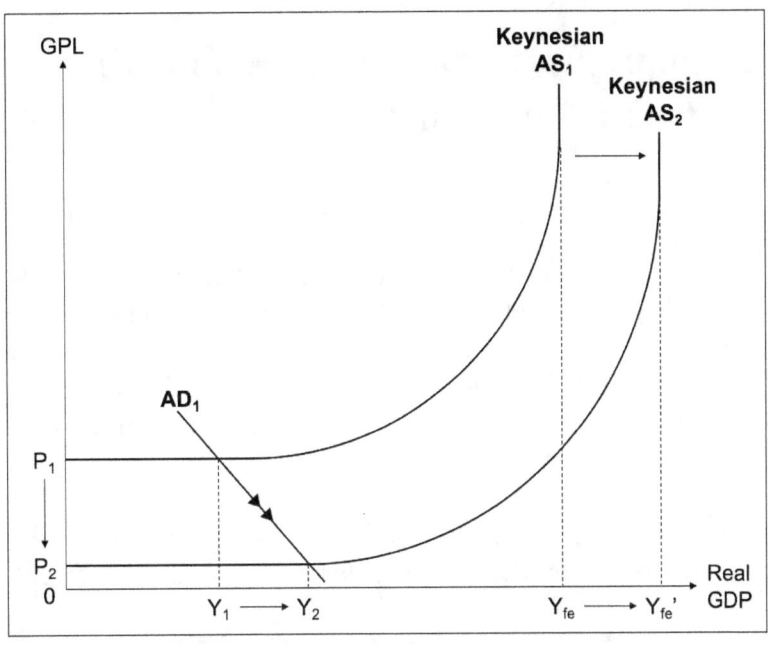

5. Also, the labour market reforms would decrease the unit costs of production of goods and services, hence increasing the expected rates of returns of investment projects. Investments (I) increase and since I is a component of AD, an increase in I would directly lead to an increase in AD from AD_1 to AD_2.

6. Referring to the diagram below, an increase in AD would cause the real output of the economy to increase from Y_1 to Y_2, leading to EG.

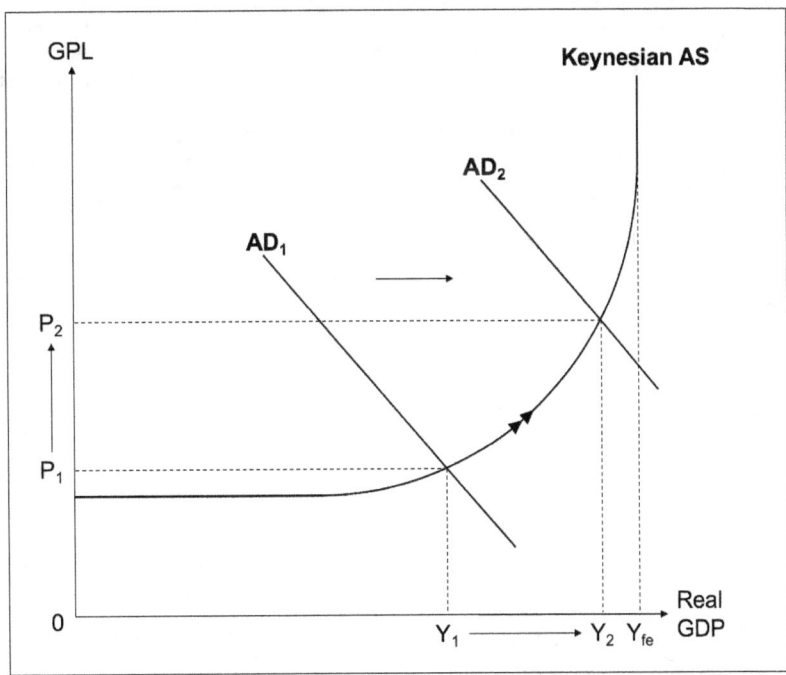

6. Using an appropriate diagram, explain why a country might experience a deflationary gap. (10)

Introduction

1. A deflationary gap occurs when the equilibrium national income of an economy is less than the full employment level of income, due to weak aggregate demand.

2. Aggregate demand (AD) is defined as the total expenditure on domestically produced goods and services in a given time period, usually a year, from all possible buyers, such as households, firms, government, and foreigners.

3. Aggregate Supply (AS) refers to the total quantity of final goods and services that would be produced in an economy over a particular time period, at different price levels, ceteris paribus.

4. Macroeconomic equilibrium occurs when AD intersects AS.

Explanation

1. A country might experience a deflationary gap due to decreases in the AD.

2. Initially the economy is at its long run equilibrium, producing at Y_{fe} and at a general price level (GPL) of P_1, as seen in the diagram below.

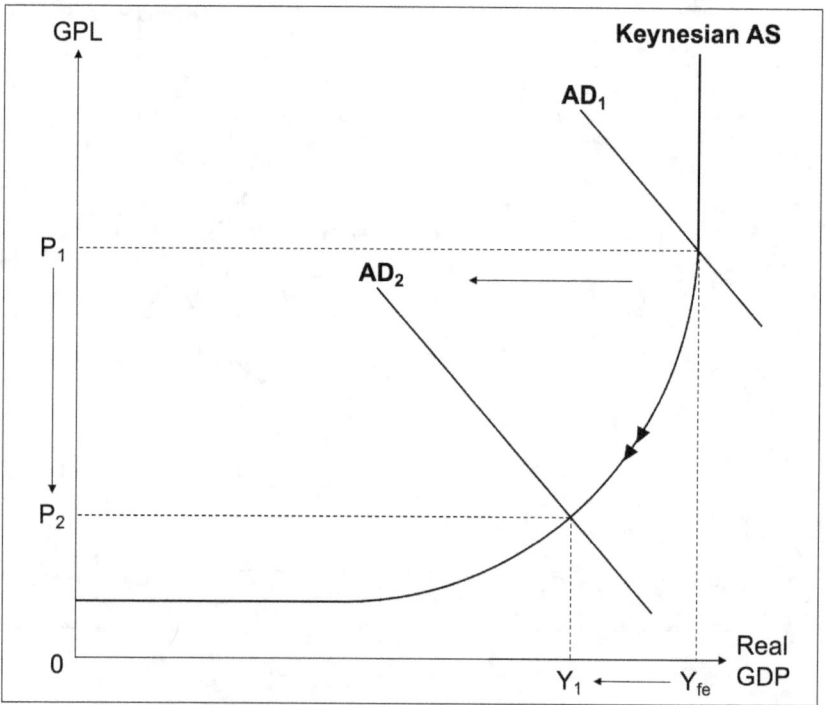

3. However, due to a decrease in Aggregate Demand, AD falls from AD_1 to AD_2 Consequently, this creates a surplus at the original price level P_1, placing a downward pressure on GPL towards P_2. The decreased price level disincentivises firms from producing, thereby causing the real output to decrease from Y_{fe} to Y_1.Thus, a deflationary gap of Y_1Y_{fe} is formed in the short-run. With this deflationary gap, there exists spare capacity in the economy, since firms require fewer resources for their production.

4. For example, the US experienced a deflationary gap during the 2008 Great Recession. During this period, consumer and business confidence plummeted, as both consumers and firms became increasingly pessimistic about the outlook of the economy. Consequently, they cut back on consumer (C) and investment (I) expenditure, both components of AD. This caused the scenario outlined above to occur, where the decrease in AD caused the US economy to experience a deflationary gap in the short-run, lasting the duration of the recession.

5. As wages are sticky downwards, due to minimum wage regulations, trade unions' resistance and fixed wage contracts, the economy does not experience a reduction in wage and unit cost of production that would increase the SRAS and adjust the economy back to Y_{fe}. Hence, the economy remains at Ye and experiences a deflationary gap.

7. With the use of short-run and long-run Phillips curves, explain how the economy will always return to the natural rate of unemployment following an increase in domestic consumption. (10)

<u>Introduction</u>

1. The Phillips curves are a neoclassical economic model concerned with describing the relationship between inflation and unemployment.

2. In the short run, there is a negative relationship between inflation and unemployment. This is reflected in the shape of the Short-Run Phillips Curve (SPRC), which is curved and convex with respect to the origin.

3. On the other hand, in the long-run, the level of unemployment in the economy is fixed at the Natural Rate of Unemployment (NRU) regardless of inflation. This is seen through the shape of the Long-Run Phillips Curve (LRPC), which is vertical.

4. The NRU refers to the unemployment rate in the economy when it is operating at full-employment output level.

<u>Diagrammatic Explanation</u>

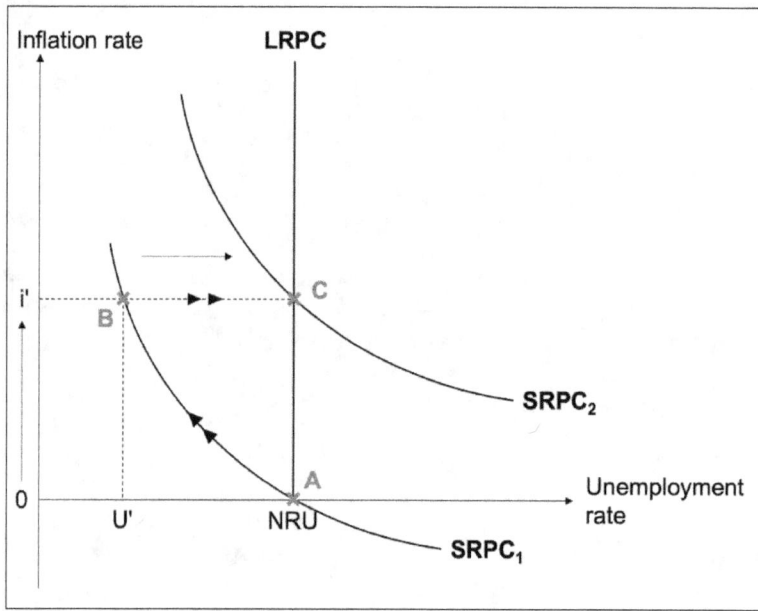

1. Assuming the economy is originally operating at full-employment output level (Y_{fe}), the unemployment rate in the economy would be NRU, by definition. With no changes in AD or SRAS, the inflation rate in the economy would be at 0%. The economy is operating at point A along $SRPC_1$ and LRPC.

2. Following an increase in domestic consumption, which constitutes one of the components of AD, Aggregate Demand will increase.

3. In the short-run, costs of production are fixed, especially labour costs. Consequently, the increase in AD leads to an increase in real output beyond Y_{fe}, for example by exploiting labour factors to work overtime and hence produce more real output. The economy experiences an inflationary gap, wherein the economy is expanding and unemployment is falling.

4. The economy moves along the $SRPC_1$ curve from point A to point B, now operating at an inflation rate i' greater than 0, and an unemployment rate u' less than the NRU.

5. However, in the long-run, factor prices become increasingly flexible. In this scenario, workers begin to demand for higher hourly wages as a result of having to work overtime and sacrifice leisure. Thus, labour costs will rise, and this would translate to an increased cost of production, which will see firms cutting back on the real output produced. Hence, unemployment rates will rise again as the economy returns to producing at full-employment output level.

6. The increased labour costs are reflected by an outward shift of the Short-Run Phillips Curve from $SRPC_1$ to $SRPC_2$. As unemployment levels rise, the economy moves from point B along $SRPC_1$ to point C along $SRPC_2$ and LRPC, causing unemployment to return to NRU.

7. Therefore, the economy will always operate along LRPC in the long-run, indicating a return to NRU.

8. Discuss the view that deflation is a more serious problem than inflation for the economy of a country. (15)

Introduction

1. Deflation is the decrease in the GPL of an economy over time.

2. Both inflation and deflation could be due to demand-side and/or supply-side factors.

3. One of the macroeconomic objectives of governments is maintaining a low and stable rate of inflation.

Thesis 1: Deflation is usually accompanied by recession

1. The Japanese economy has been experiencing bouts of deflation for the past two decades. From 2000 – 2005, deflation was at 0.5% annually, and from 2009 – 2012 deflation worsened to 2% annually owing to the global recession.

2. In Japan's case, deflation was due to demand-side factors, namely weak or falling Aggregate Demand (AD).

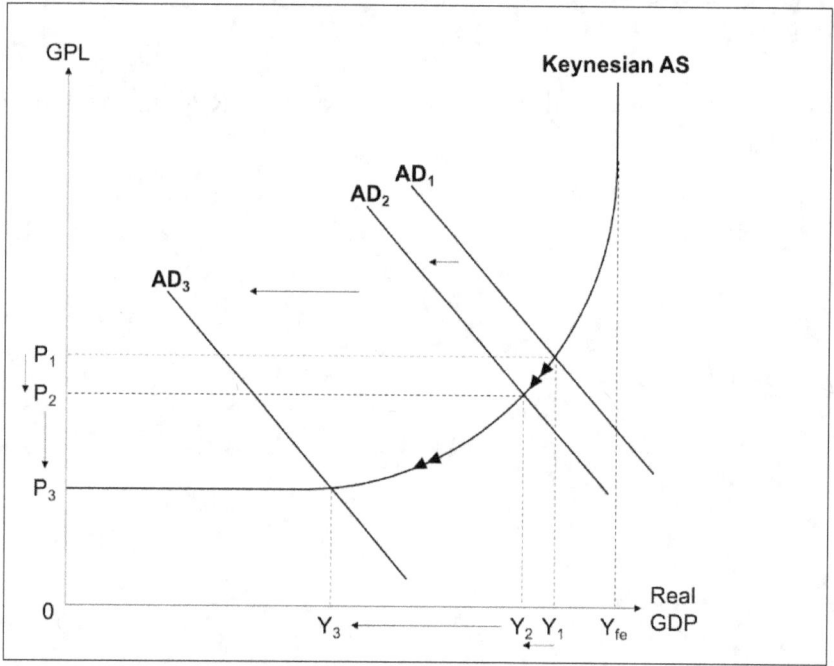

3. This is represented as a decrease in AD from AD_1 to AD_2. This creates a surplus at the original price level P_1, which places a downward (deflationary) pressure on GPL towards P_2. Consequently, this incentivises Japanese firms to reduce their real output from Y_1 to Y_2 – placing a recessionary pressure on the economy.

4. As a result, Japanese firms require fewer units of factor inputs, one of them being labour. This reduces the derived demand for labour which, in turn, increases demand-deficient unemployment.Thus, standard of living, both materially (through fall in income and consumption) and non-materially (for example, through greater stress due to income loss) falls.

5. Cost-push inflation can also lead to recession.

6. For example, the OPEC oil embargo on the US in 1973 caused a significant and sudden increase in the price of oil, from US$3 a barrel to US$12 a barrel.

7. Since oil is a widely-used factor input in the production of most goods and services, such significant increases in the price of oil translate to increased unit cost of production for firms in the economy.

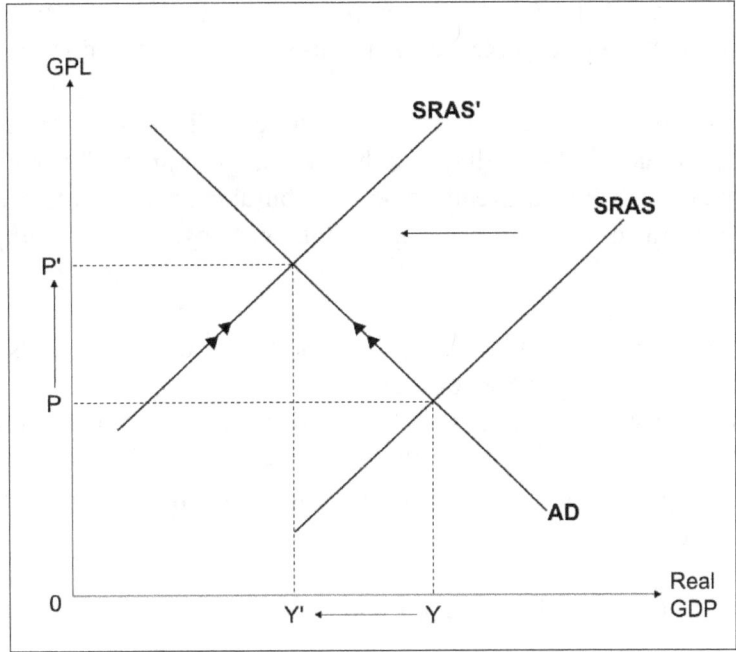

8. Short-run aggregate supply decreases from SRAS to SRAS'. This creates a shortage at the original price level P, placing an upward pressure on price levels towards P', constituting cost-push inflation.

9. Simultaneously, however, real national output falls from Y to Y'.

Thesis 2: Risk of a deflationary spiral

1. The economy may be a stuck in a deflationary spiral, accompanied by recessions or stagnant growth, as is evident in Japan's case, where deflationary pressures have been so prolonged over recent years, that economists now term the phenomenon as "Japan's Two Lost Decades".

2. The spiralling effect occurs since current patterns of deflation create the expectation that prices will fall in the future, encouraging consumers to postpone their purchases so as to obtain them at a lower price in the near future. This leads to reduced consumption expenditure by households.

3. Additionally, those who are retrenched and have lost their sources of income are also likely to cut back on consumption, since their disposable incomes have plummeted.

4. Firms are also disincentivised from investing (I), since while prices of goods and services are falling, the unit costs of production may not be falling due to various reasons that lead to wage stickiness. This reduces profit margins and hence decreases firms' expected rate of returns on Investment projects, and therefore firms are likely to decrease I.

5. There may also be a cutting back of government expenditure (G). This is because, as incomes and consumption falls, governments now collect less in tax revenue (through income taxes, consumption taxes, etc), and have less funds to finance expenditure.

6. Prolonged deflation could also lead to bankruptcies. This is because, although prices are falling, the nominal (dollar) value of debt remains the same. This causes the real value of debt to increase, placing a greater financial burden on consumers and firms who have previously borrowed money. Debt repayments will cost more, causing less to be spent on C and I.

7. These effects perpetuate a vicious cycle – the initial deflation leads to decreases in C, I and G. As these are components of AD, this further reduces AD from AD_2 to AD_3, causing further deflationary pressures (P_2 to P_3) and reduction in real national output (Y_2 to Y_3).

8. This exacerbates the previously-mentioned negative impacts on growth, unemployment and SOL.

Thesis 3: Low and steady inflation is good

1. Low and steady rates of demand-pull inflation is a sign of a growing economy with increasing AD.

2. From the diagram below, this scenario can be seen through the increases in AD from AD_1 to AD_2, creating a shortage at the original price level P_1 that places a slight upward pressure on prices towards P_2. This, in turn, incentivises firms to increase their real output from Y_1 to Y_2.

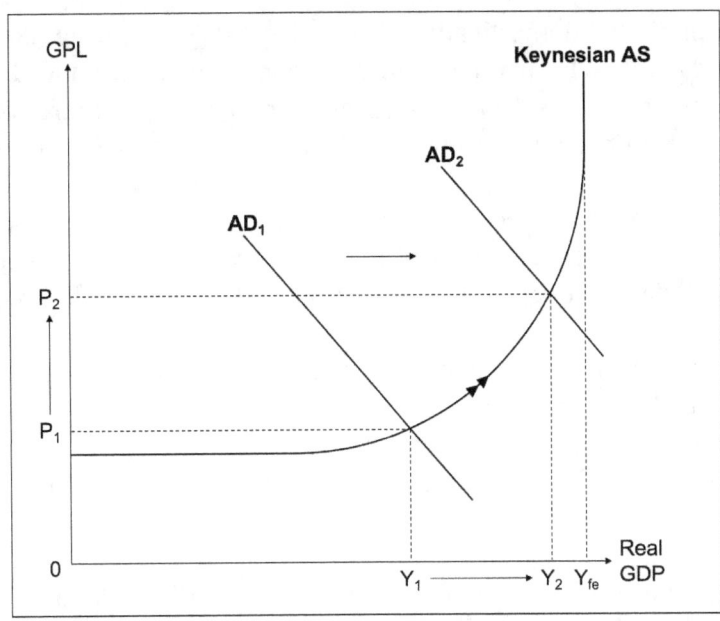

3. Clearly, this is a scenario of positive economic growth, falling unemployment and increasing standard of living.

4. In addition, as the costs of production may be lagging behind the increase in prove levels due to for example, fixed wage contracts, profit margins rise, and the incentive to invest increases. This in turn can spur more economic growth, both actual and potential.

Anti-Thesis 1: Adverse Consequences of Inflation

1. High rates of inflation could lead to severe detrimental consequences.

2. Demand-pull inflation could worsen the distribution of income since fixed-wage earners will see the real value of their wages falling. Fixed-wage earners refer to salaried employees receiving a set dollar figure per hour of work; this primarily constitutes low-income minimum wage earners. With goods and services becoming more expensive while their incomes remain constant, these fixed-wage earners will face a decreasing standard of living.

3. In comparison, variable-wage earners are likely to see their nominal wages rising to outpace the rate of inflation in the economy, allowing their real wages to increase. Variable-wage earners are workers whose wages change based on economic outlook, including business owners and entrepreneurs, or top management workers receiving bonuses. Therefore, the standard of living of these earners will rise.

4. This leads to inequity, as low-income, fixed-wage earners will be worse off due to inflation, whereas high-income, variable-wage earners will benefit.

5. Furthermore, inflation could possibly lead to a negative effect on the country's trade balance and hence balance of payments (BOP).

6. The higher prices of domestically produced goods and services will result in imports becoming relatively cheaper compared to domestically produced goods and services. Hence, assuming imports and domestically produced goods are substitutes, consumers will increase their demand for imports, increasing import expenditure.

7. Simultaneously, exports become relatively more expensive as compared to foreign produced goods and services. Hence, exports lose competitiveness and foreigners reduce quantity demanded for exports.

8. With an increase in import expenditure and a reduction in export revenue, the country's BOT and hence BOP deteriorates.

9. On the other hand, deflation can lead to a positive effect on a country's trade balance, and hence the country's BOP.

10. For example, during the Asian Financial Crisis of 1997, the Thai economy faced low levels of AD, leading to deflation.

11. This deflation lowered the price of Thai exports (such as rice and other agricultural products) relative to its trading partners, who were less badly hit by the crisis and thus did not experience such severe deflation. As a result, these other countries switched to consuming Thai rice, over the relatively more expensive rice produced locally or imported from elsewhere. Therefore, the export revenue (X) earned by Thailand increased.

12. Simultaneously, the deflation in Thailand caused imports of foreign products to become relatively more expensive to the Thai people. Therefore, the Thais switched from consuming imports to consuming to the relatively cheaper locally-produced goods. This caused the import expenditure (M) by Thailand to decrease.

13. This increase in X and decrease in M caused a net positive change to the balance of trade. Consequently, the balance of payments would also improve, ceteris paribus.

Anti-Thesis 2: Hyperinflation is worse than deflation

1. This is demonstrated through the case of Zimbabwe, with an inflation rate of 79.6 billion % per month in Nov 2008. This meant that prices doubled every 3.5 milliseconds, with the price of one good in the evening costing 1.33 billion times as much as it did in the morning.

2. The effect of this is catastrophic. In the span of a day, people's life savings are eliminated as the real value of their savings plummets to virtually zero. Banks and financial institutions collapse as the real value of their loans decreases to zero, and people no longer deposit money.

3. Firms are unwilling to sell goods whose prices (in the local currency) are constantly changing. Firms shut down as people refuse to work in jobs whose real wages are virtually zero.

4. Shortages, especially in daily necessities like soap, food and clothing, are rampant and there is widespread social unrest as transactions become a matter of barter trade. Theft and looting become rampant as many who are unable to get their hands on daily necessities resort instead to desperate measures.

5. By this time, few/no government policies could correct the economy. They simply act too slowly to correct the hyperinflation.

6. In fact, the government itself is unable to finance its day-to-day operations. Similarly, the central bank is incapable of printing money fast enough to keep up at the rate with which its real value is falling.

7. Hyperinflation could thus very well lead to an economic collapse and is far worse than any problems arising from deflation.

<u>Anti-Thesis 3: Deflation can be good, too</u>

1. Deflation can have beneficial effects if it were due to supply-side factors.

2. For example, from 2008 to 2016, crude oil prices worldwide have been on a downward trend – from a peak of US$161.23 per barrel in June 2008 to a low of US$30.29 in Jan 2016.

3. Since oil is a widely-used factor input in the production of many goods and services, a decrease in oil prices would lead to a decrease in the unit cost of production of firms in the economy.

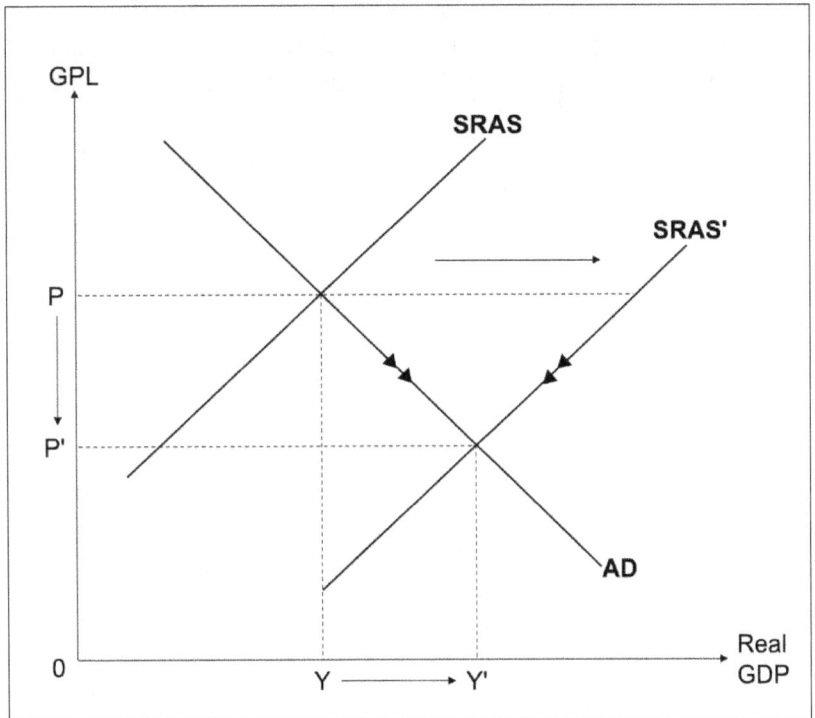

4. Consequently, firms would enjoy greater profits margins, incentivising them to increase their production from SRAS to SRAS'. This creates a surplus at the original price level P, placing a downward pressure on prices towards P', constituting deflation.

5. A similar scenario could occur owing to technological advancements. For example, the rise of automation has streamlined production processes, lowering the costs of production of many goods and services in the economy. This improvement in productivity leads to increases in AS, lowering prices and leading to increased growth.

6. The economy enjoys growth from Y to Y' and decreased demand-deficient unemployment, leading to higher material standard of living.

7. These benefits of deflation outweigh the consequences of deflation as discussed above.

Concluding Section

1. Whether the severity of one outweighs the other depends on several factors.

2. For one, the causes of deflation and inflation matter. Cost-push inflation and demand-pull deflation tends to be more detrimental and are thus more serious problems.

3. It is also pertinent to consider the extent of deflation/inflation concerned. Uncontrolled inflation (as in Zimbabwe's case) and prolonged deflation (as in Japan's case) both carry serious consequences. However, the former is a more serious problem given that the entire economy practically collapses.

4. Finally, governments tend to fear having to tackle deflation as policies to deal with deflation tend to be less effective than policies aimed at curbing inflation. For example, expansionary monetary policy to increase AD and GPL. However, interest rates cannot really fall below zero, whereas to tackle inflation, interest rates can keep increasing.

5. Thus, the ideal for any economy would be to achieve a low and stable rate of inflation.

9. Evaluate the view that attempts to achieve greater equity in the distribution of income will reduce economic efficiency. (15)

Introduction

1. The problem of income inequality arises because ownership of factors of production (FOPs) are highly unequal in the free market system, resulting in vast inequality in factor incomes resulting in some with little or no access to basic necessities.

2. Therefore, the pursuit of equity in the distribution of income is the pursuit for greater equality relative to what would be achieved by the free market system.

3. This could be achieved through a variety of government policies such as progressive taxation, income redistribution through subsidies and transfer payments, price and wage controls.

4. Economic efficiency includes both productive and allocative efficiency. Productive efficiency refers to the scenario in which the economy is producing at its maximum possible output fully and efficiently utilising all available resources. Allocative efficiency refers to the economy producing the combination of goods most wanted by society.

Policy 1: Progressive Taxation

1. To promote greater equality in income distribution and thus equity, progressive taxation could be used as a tool to narrow income differences between the rich and the poor.

2. Progressive taxation refers to a system of direct taxation by which high income taxpayers pay a larger proportion of their income than low income taxpayers.

3. Progressive taxation significantly reduces the disposable income of the rich with little no change to the income of the poor (should their income be low enough to be exempted from tax).

4. For example, the UK charges a 45% tax rate on incomes earned above £150,000. However, the government allows for a deductible "personal allowance" amount of £11,850, for which no tax is charged. Should someone earn £11,850 a year or less, they would not need to pay income taxes.

5. To further narrow income differences, such progressive taxation could also be extended to capital gains and interest incomes earned by the rich.

<u>Policy 1: Negative Impact on Efficiency</u>

1. If progressive taxation is too high, it may result in people trying to evade taxes.

2. For example, the UK was infamous for implementing its "supertax" in the late 20th Century, which caused the effective tax rate on the highest-income earners to reach 95%.

3. This created a disincentive to work among the wealthy. Given that most of the additional income they would earn from working harder would be taxed by the government, they faced little motivation to work harder and to earn more.

4. Consequently, this disincentive to work is likely to result in under-utilisation of labour: namely underemployment leading to productive inefficiency.

5. This is as illustrated in the diagram below, where the economy is operating at point A, within its production possibilities curve (PPC).

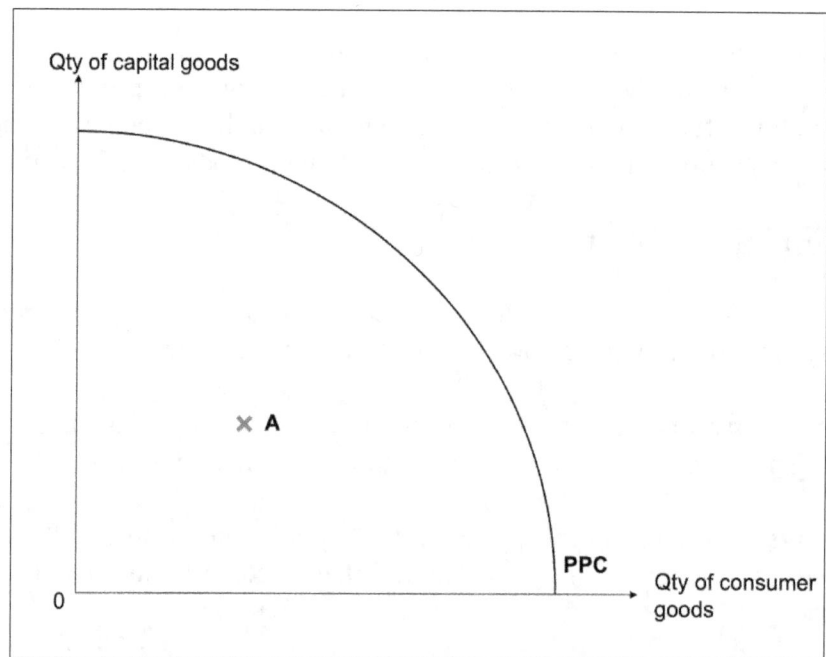

6. As a result, while equity is achieved, it comes at the expense of productive and allocative efficiency.

<u>Policy 2: Subsidies and Transfer Payments</u>

1. Governments often use the tax revenues accrued from progressive taxation to fund subsidies and transfer payments. These are efforts to redistribute the income – taxing the rich and distributing it to the poor. For example, the government could subsidise the provision of merit goods.

Policy 2: Positive Effect on Allocative Efficiency

1. Merit goods are goods deemed by the government to be socially desirable owing to the positive externalities they generate.

2. For example, education generates positive externalities, since increased levels of education allow for a more productive workforce, driving economic growth that increases the income levels of others in the economy. Therefore this causes a divergence between MPB and MSB, such that MSB > MPB at each and every Q, the difference of which constitutes MEC.

3. The free market transacts at Qe, where MPB = MPC, however at this level MSB > MSC. The socially optimal quantity is at Qs, where MSB = MSC. There is hence an under-consumption of education by the amount Qs - Qe.

4. This under-consumption is worsened by the fact that not everyone can afford to pay the equilibrium price Pe to afford education. Many who are poor live paycheque to paycheque, struggling to even put food on the table.

5. The market has failed to achieve allocative efficiency, under-allocating resources to education. This results in a subsequent welfare loss (potential welfare gain) as illustrated in the diagram.

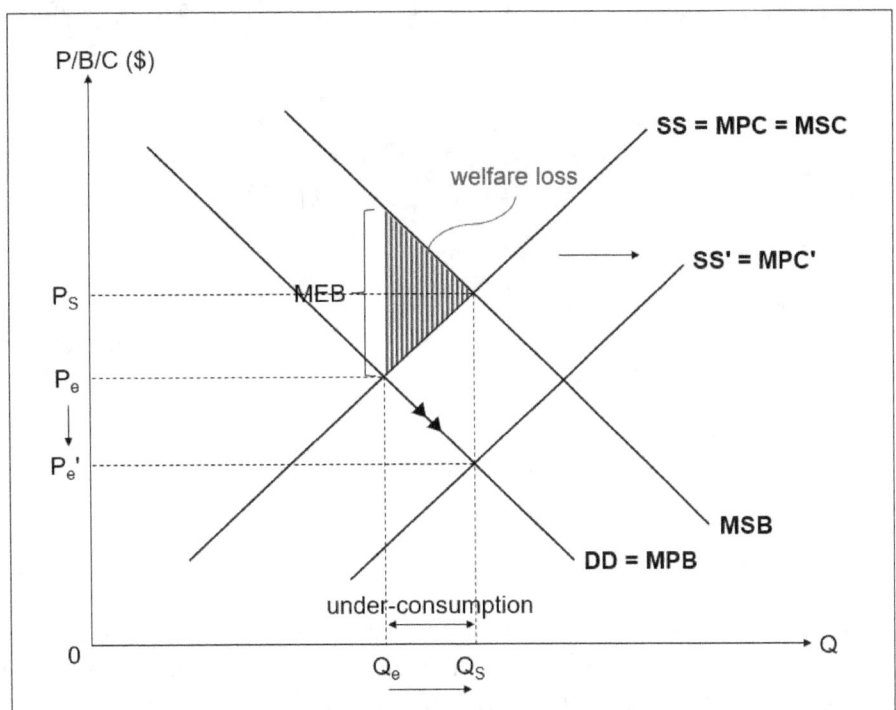

6. Therefore, the government could subsidise education, at a level of subsidy per unit = MEB. This results in an increase in supply (and a decrease in MPC) from SS to SS', increasing quantity consumed from Qe to Qs, the socially optimal level.

7. For example, in Singapore, all citizens are able to enjoy subsidised primary and secondary education at public schools, allowing all (regardless of income levels) to enjoy education.

8. This hence achieves allocative efficiency in the market for education, allowing the socially-optimal quantity of education to be produced, while serving to increase equity by allowing all a fair chance to receive education.

9. This is especially important in allowing one to break out of the poverty cycle, as increased education leads to a more highly-skilled labour which allows for increased incomes in the future.

<u>Policy 2: Negative Effect on Allocative Efficiency</u>

1. However, there is the risk of government failure, in which the government over-estimates the subsidy amount required.

2. For example, Nordic countries such as Finland offer fully-subsidised, free-of-charge education at primary, secondary and tertiary levels, to all including foreigners.

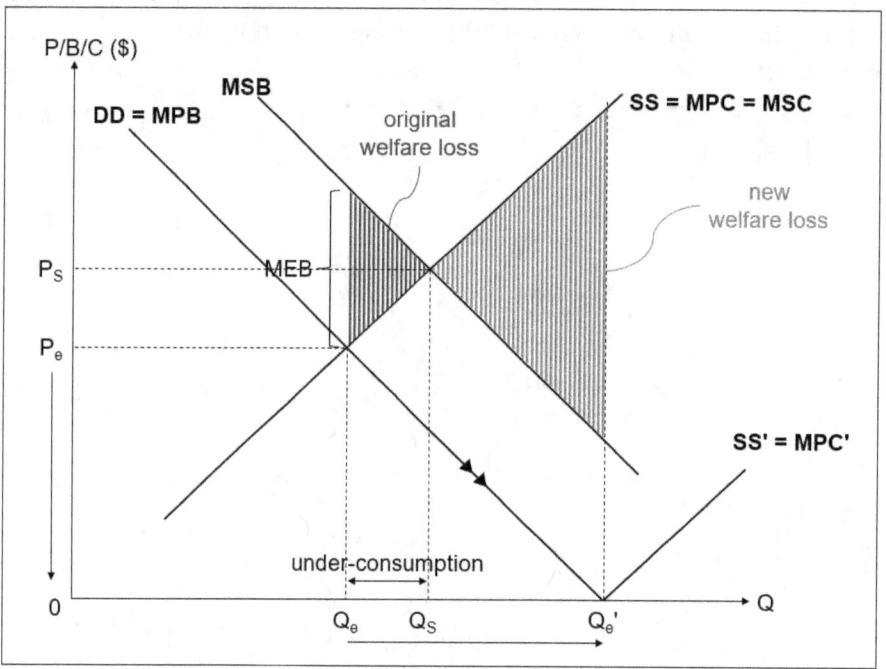

3. This could, in fact, worsen the allocative inefficiency – by increasing Supply until the equilibrium price is zero, this causes education to be over-consumed by the amount Q_e'-Q_s, which is even larger than the original under-consumption of Q_s - Q_e. This creates a new welfare loss that is substantially greater than the original one.

4. In the case of Finland, this over-consumption and new welfare loss to society manifests itself in the abuse of free education. Many Finnish citizens overstay in school, delaying their entrance into the labour force. Some even find working too difficult, and would instead choose to continue pursuing studies beyond the point of redundancy (for example, accumulating multiple bachelor's degrees in different courses).

5. Such an extreme policy would be achieving equity at the expense of allocative efficiency.

Policy 3: Minimum Wage

1. A minimum wage refers to a legally-imposed price floor in the labour market, ensuring that all workers receive at least a given wage per hour. For example, in the US, there is federal minimum wage of US$ 7.25 per hour.

2. The minimum wage is particularly of concern in the market for low-skilled labour, where the equilibrium wage (W_e) would be below the minimum wage imposed. This hence serves to increase the wages of low-skilled, low-income workers, allowing them to enjoy a wage that allows them to afford basic necessities such as housing, thereby improving equity. W_{min}, as seen in the diagram below, represents the legal minimum wage set by the government.

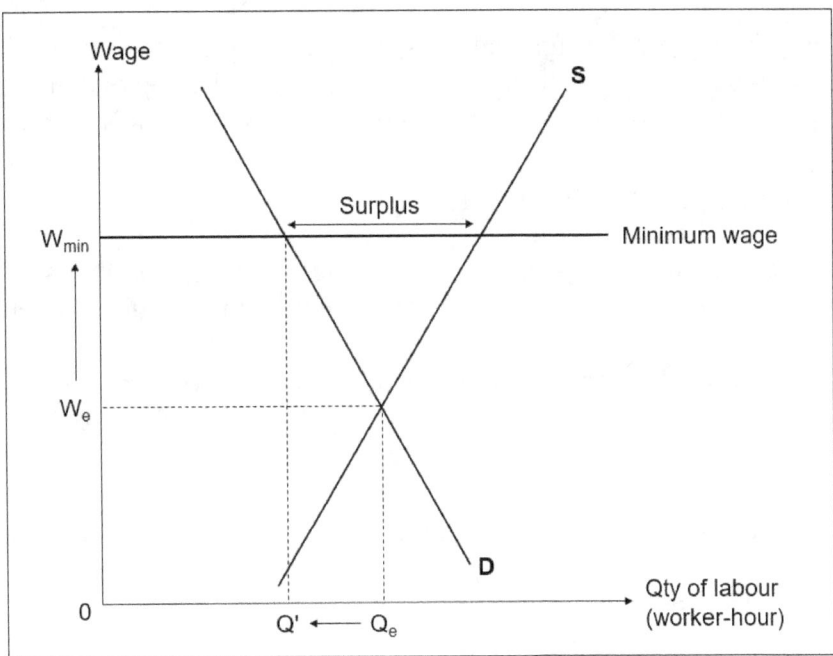

3. In this market for low-skilled labour, minimum wage creates a permanent surplus of labour as seen in the diagram above, as the quantity demanded of labour decreases while the quantity supplied of labour increases.

4. The total amount of labour employed decreases from Qe to Q'.

Policy 3: Negative impact on efficiency

1. Since the minimum wage fundamentally results in a decrease in the quantity of labour employed, this means that some workers may be retrenched or have their working hours reduced.

2. For workers retrenched, they are likely to be even worse off as they receive no income. The surplus of workers as seen in the diagram above represents unemployment. Since labour is a factor of production (FOP), unemployment would mean that the economy is productive inefficient since FOPs are idle.

3. This leads to a net welfare loss to society as indicated on the diagram above. This translates to reduced allocative efficiency, as too few workers are allocated jobs, and reduced productive efficiency, as some workers are left without a job.

Policy 3: Positive impact on efficiency

1. For one, research studies have demonstrated that low wages cause workers to engage in 'shirking', or doing less work than they are capable of doing - a form of underemployment.

2. Therefore, the increased wage and prospects of being retrenched would motivate these workers to work harder, reducing the incidence of underemployment, and consequently allowing labour factors to be more productive, increasing productive efficiency.

Policy 4: Training for low-skilled workers

1. Supply-side policies, in particular providing training for low-skilled, low-income workers, is also a means of ensuring greater equity in income distribution.

2. By providing subsidies for such training to low-income workers, these workers would be able to increase their skillsets and thus their employability. This would allow them to find a better-paying job in the future, which therefore allows them to earn increased wages.

3. One example would be the Workfare Training Support Scheme implemented by the Singapore government. The scheme provides subsidies and allowances for low-income workers to attend skills-upgrading courses. These are targeted at workers earning a gross monthly income below S$ 2000.

Policy 4: Positive effect on efficiency

1. Providing low-income workers with training helps to alleviate possible issues of structural employment. As low-income workers are typically performing jobs wherein little knowledge is required, such jobs are increasingly becoming obsolete, being replaced by automation. Consequently, such training is critical in ensuring that these workers will be able to find alternative jobs thus maintaining productive efficiency of the economy.

2. Additionally, there are positive externalities involved with the training of workers. This is because the consumption of such training allows for a more highly-skilled workforce that is more productive and leads to improved economic growth for the society as a whole. Consequently, if left to the free market, training would be under-consumed. Therefore, this supply-side policy would allow for the quantity of worker training undertaken to be increased towards the socially-optimal level, moving towards efficient allocation of resources to training.

Concluding Section

1. Therefore, when aiming to implement policies to improve equity, the government needs to consider the repercussions it might have on efficiency. There is a trade-off between the two.

2. There are definitely instances of a trade-off between equity and economic efficiency, although there are also instances whereby achieving greater equity unequivocally promotes efficiency.

3. Where trade-offs exist, it is important for the government to weigh the costs and benefits to ensure that the overall outcome is an increase in society's welfare. For example, whether the implementation of a minimum wage would serve to motivate workers more so than the layoffs that the policy may cause.

4. To minimise the trade-offs, the government also has to carefully calibrate the extent of progressivity in income taxes, as well as subsidies. Perhaps the training of low-income workers should be favoured over a minimum wage law.

10. Discuss the view that economic growth always leads to a more equal distribution of income and a reduction in unemployment. (15)

Introduction

1. Economic growth can be achieved in 2 aspects: actual growth and potential growth.

2. Actual growth is the annual percentage increase in national output actually produced which can be achieved by an increase in the Aggregate Demand or an increase in the short-run aggregate supply (SRAS) of the economy.

3. Potential growth refers to the increase in the amount of output the economy could produce if all resources are utilised, which occurs with an increase in the long-run aggregate supply (LRAS).

Thesis 1: EG reduces UE

1. Firstly, economic growth (EG) can lead to a reduction in unemployment (UE) and a more equal distribution of income if the government has implemented redistributive measures, such as a progressive income tax structure and welfare benefits.

2. The increasing real national income means that more households will enter into higher tax brackets and pay higher percentages of their income in the form of taxes.

3. The increase in taxes collected would enable the government to fund welfare programmes that provide subsidies and transfer payments to supplement the income of poorer households, thus enabling a faster rise in their disposable income.

4. For example, Singapore's Workfare Training Support scheme provides subsidies for workers with a monthly income of less than $2000 to attend skill-upgrading courses, creating productive employment opportunities for them and enabling them to earn higher incomes. Also, the recent Goods and Services Tax (GST) vouchers distributed by the Singapore government are targeted at lower income households, which reduces the tax burden placed on them, thereby increasing their purchasing power for basic necessities.

5. In addition, as firms are producing more output, there will be an increase in the derived demand for labour, leading to more workers employed and a fall in derived demand unemployment.

6. This also helps promote a more equal income distribution since those who were previously jobless and earning zero income may now obtain a job and earn an income.

Anti-Thesis 1: EG may not benefit low-income earners

1. Economic growth may not lead to a more equal distribution of income. It depends on what is driving the economic growth.

2. For example, in the case export-led growth, assuming demand for a country's exports is increasing, the main beneficiaries of the growth would be from the export sectors. If there is originally a higher concentration of high-income earners in the export sectors, such economic growth would thus worsen income inequality.

3. Similarly, if the economic growth is mainly capital-driven, there would not be significant reduction in unemployment and the benefits of the economic growth would likely be concentrated in the hands of capital owners which would in the first place be among the high-income earners.

4. Such economic growth is not broad-based and hence not inclusive and would not lead to a more equal income distribution.

Anti-Thesis 2: EG might not reduce / may even worsen structural UE

1. EG may not lead to a reduction in structural unemployment. Structural unemployment is usually caused by a mismatch between the skills workers possess and what employers want.

2. Economic growth, while leading to an increase in real national output and thus job vacancies, may involve an increase in demand of skills which the unemployed lack.

3. For example, the hard drive industry is a sunset industry in Singapore, and many workers in this industry have been retrenched in recent years. Despite high levels of EG enjoyed by the Singaporean economy, most jobs have been created in booming 'sunrise' industries such as biomedicine. A retrenched worker from the hard drive industry, lacking the skills in increasing demand by biomedical firms, would remain structurally unemployed in spite of EG. In this case, EG does little to reduce structural UE.

4. If as earlier mentioned, the economic growth is capital-driven, there could be accompanied technological advancement that leads to the displacement of workers, increasing structural unemployment instead. For example, the development of cashless payment technology would cause service workers in fast food chains to become obsolete as self-payment kiosks are increasingly used to replace them. In this instance, EG would in fact lead to these service workers losing their jobs, creating/worsening structural UE.

5. In turn, this would also worsen the distribution of income. Low-income, low-skilled workers are more likely to face structural UE due to EG. Being retrenched, these workers now have no income, and may have to rely solely on their limited savings to purchase daily necessities. Some might even have to go without necessities. EG this disproportionately affects the lower-income brackets of society.

Anti Thesis 3: EG might worsen frictional UE

1. Additionally, EG can also worsen the problem of frictional unemployment, caused by imperfect labour market information.

2. Ironically, the increased number of jobs available enables the paradox of choice, in which workers looking for jobs now spend a longer time researching amongst the larger volume of work available and thus take longer to find employment.

Concluding Section

1. In conclusion, whether or not EG leads to a more equal income distribution depends significantly on the sources of growth and whether the government implements income redistributive policies.

2. It also depends on how the government utilises the increase in tax revenues arising from growth. If training programs are funded, structural unemployment can be reduced. Thus, economic growth may not directly achieve those outcomes but increases the ability of the government to achieve them.

11. Discuss the view that an economy will always return to the full employment equilibrium level of output in the long run. (15)

Introduction

1. There are two main competing theories about the macroeconomy.

2. Neoclassical, or Monetarist theory, holds that the economy always returns to the full-employment output level in the long run. There can be short-term changes in the output level, above or below the full-employment output level, but this will not persist.

3. On the other hand, Keynesian theory holds that the economy will not 'automatically' return to the full-employment output level in the long run; government intervention is often required for this to happen. On the other hand, economic output can remain below full-employment level for extended periods of time.

Thesis: Explanation of neoclassical theory

1. Neoclassical theory makes an important distinction between short-run and long-run.

2. In the short-run, factor prices remain the same and there may be output gaps (difference between actual output and full employment level of output). However, in the long-run, factor prices become fully flexible, and this allows for the economy to enter a 'self-correcting' state, eliminating any deflationary or inflationary gaps.

3. Therefore, any changes in the level of AD will only influence the General Price Level (GPL), and not the real output, in the long-run. Consequently, in the long-run, the aggregate supply curve best approximates a vertical line at the full-employment output level (Y_{fe}), a curve known as the Long Run Aggregate Supply (LRAS).

4. For example, economic growth overseas could have led to an increase in demand for exports, increasing net exports and thus Aggregate Demand (AD), ceteris paribus.

5. With the increase in AD, there will be an increase in real output in the short run, from Y_{fe} to Y_1. This increase in real output is possible, for instance by making existing workers work overtime and paying them extra, even though the economy was originally employing all resources available. However, in the long run, wages will adjust upwards as workers will demand for higher hourly rates to compensate for their loss of leisure and as general price levels have risen, unions demand for higher wages to keep real incomes constant. This leads to increased unit labour costs of production, causing the Short-Run Aggregate Supply (SRAS) to decrease, bringing the economy back to equilibrium at Y_{fe}. All that has changed in the long-run, is that the GPL has increased. This scenario is delineated in the diagram on the next page.

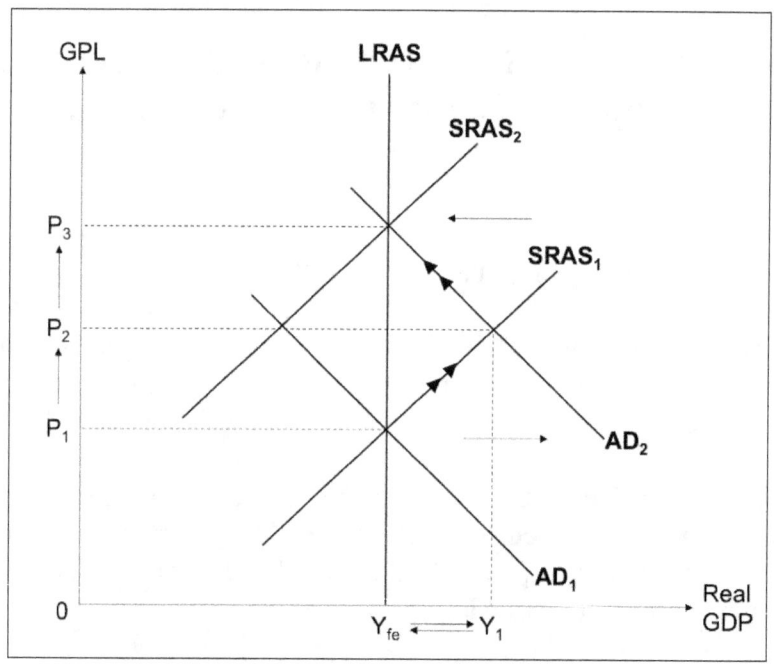

6. On the other hand, we can also consider the possibility of a falling AD, for example, due to a fall in Government spending. With the decrease in AD, there will be a decrease in real output in the short run, from Y_{fe} to Y_2 as seen in the figure below. With this decrease in production, less labour needs to be employed to satisfy the output, leading to unemployment. As workers would rather earn some income than none at all, they will be willing to accept lower wages. Falling wages would thus allow the unit costs of production to fall, thereby causing SRAS to increase, increasing real output back to Y_{fe}. All that has changed in the long-run, is that GPL has decreased. This scenario is delineated in the diagram below.

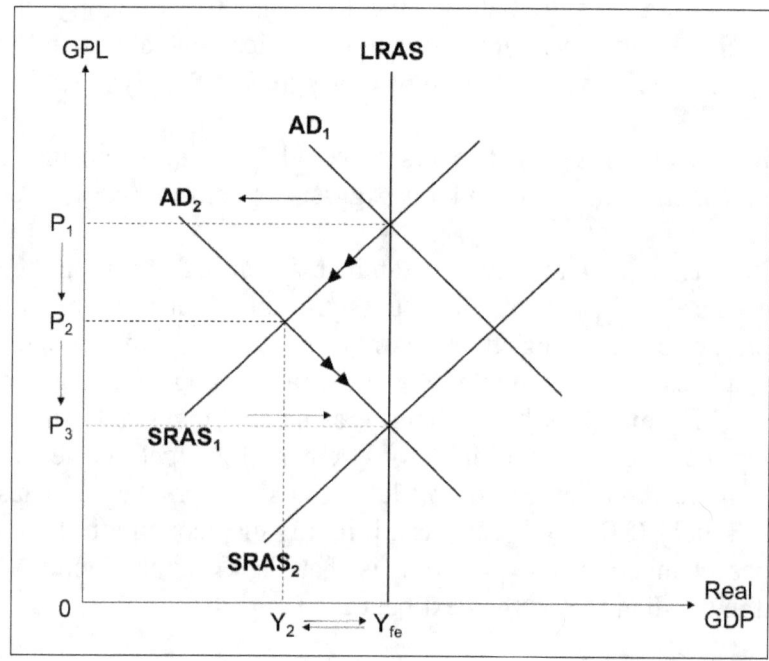

Anti-Thesis: Explanation of Keynesian theory

1. However, the neoclassical theory was found to be inadequate, when the US economy did not in fact 'self-correct' the deflationary gap it faced during the 1930s Great Depression. Recessions and unemployments persisted for years, in spite of what the leading economists at the time predicted.

2. This led to the formulation of Keynesian theory, which holds that the economy is fundamentally unable to move into the 'long-run' as postulated in the neoclassical theory. Wages and factor prices remain inflexible.

3. Wages are rigid because of long-term labour contracts between firms and workers, and trade unions which resist wage cuts, as well as the existence of minimum wage legislations. These prevented wages from falling despite unemployment. Thus, the economy persisted in a state where real output was below the full-employment output level.

4. This means that the economy may be at equilibrium at any level of real output, and will not always return to the full-employment output level.

5. Keynesian theory is best illustrated through the three sections of the Keynesian AS curve – the horizontal, upward-sloping and vertical sections. Depending on the level of AD in the economy, equilibrium positions can be found on any section of the curve, and not just at Y_{fe}.

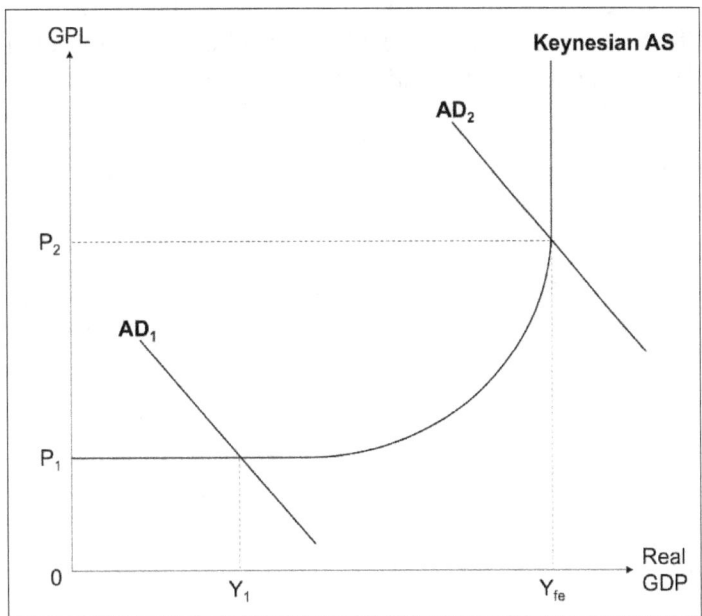

6. During the Great Depression, the US economy might be best represented by the curve AD_1, along the horizontal section of the Keynesian AS curve – where there is massive unemployment of resources. The economy attains an equilibrium output level at Y_1, with no 'self-correcting' measure which closes the deflationary gap (Y_1-Y_{fe}) automatically.

7. The only way to close the deflationary gap, and bring the economy to full-employment output level, would be to increase AD through government policies. For example, discretionary fiscal policies using increased government expenditure to boost Aggregate Demand from AD_1 to AD_2, thereby increasing real output.

8. If left up to the free market, the deflationary gap will persist indefinitely, with wages unable to fall, and the economy unable to self-correct.

Concluding Section

1. The validity of the statement in question depends on which macroeconomic theory is employed for analysis. While the neoclassical theory holds the statement to be true, Keynesian theory does not.

2. However, as elaborated previously, it does appear that the Keynesian theory holds more weight than neoclassical theory, given the experiences of a prolonged deflationary gap during the Great Depression. Hence, in real life, it appears that the economy will not always return to the full-employment output level. As Keynes famously said, "in the long-run, we are all dead" — suggesting that if Government does not intervene, one will not see the economy adjusting to full employment in one's lifetime.

3. It is also pertinent to consider the extent of wage rigidity in the economy. For example, in Singapore, there is no minimum wage and there is some variable wage component in basic wages which can be adjusted in time of recessions. Also, industrial relations are harmonious and collaborative instead of adversarial. This helps to facilitate some adjustments to Y_{fe}, meaning that the Singapore economy might more closely adhere to the predictions outlined in Neoclassical theory.

12. Evaluate the effectiveness of fiscal policy in achieving economic growth. (15)

Introduction

1. Fiscal policy (FP) usually consists of changing the level of government spending and/or the tax rates.

2. Economic growth can be achieved in 2 aspects: actual growth and potential growth.

3. Actual growth is the annual percentage increase in national output actually produced which can be triggered by an increase in any of the components of Aggregate Demand - consumption (C), investments (I), government expenditure (G), net exports (X-M). It can also be caused by an increase in the Short-Run Aggregate Supply (SRAS) of the economy.

4. Potential growth, on the other hand, refers to increases in the productive capacity of the economy, i.e. the amount of output that could be produced if all resources are fully employed. The productive capacity of the economy could be expanded due to an increase in the quantity or quality of factors of production (FOP).

Thesis 1: FP is effective in achieving economic growth.

1. Expansionary FP involves increasing of government expenditure (G). This can involve development projects to build infrastructure, or other forms of public works like road works.

2. Expansionary FP could also consist of a decrease in tax rates such as personal and corporate tax rates.

3. As G is a component of the AD, an increase in G would directly lead to an increase in AD. Additionally, the decrease in personal income tax rates means that disposable income is now higher, which leads to an increase in purchasing power and hence consumption (C).

4. Referring to the diagram on the next page, the reduction of corporate tax rates will increase the after-tax profits of firms, and hence the expected rate of return on investments. They will likely revise their expectations of the future profits and increase their level of investments (I) at each and every prevailing i/r level. As a result, demand for I increases from DD_{I1} to DD_{I2} and planned level of investments will increase from I_1 to I_2.

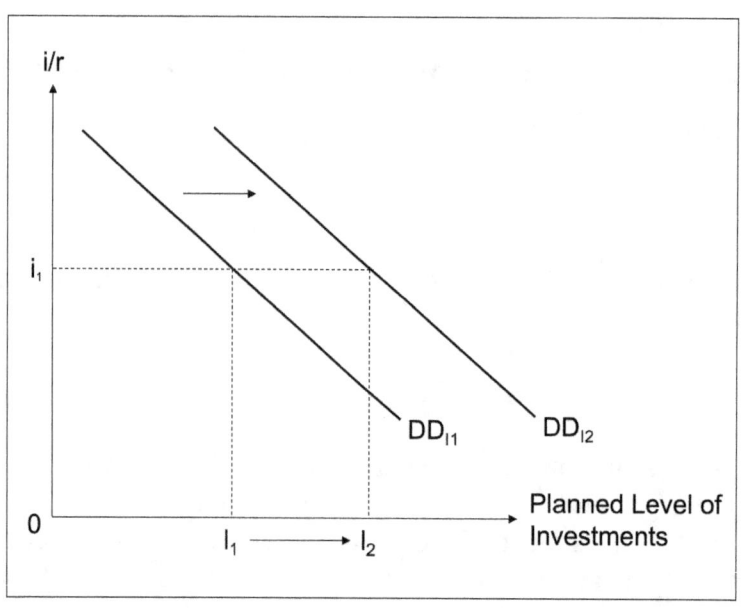

5. With an increase in C, I and G, components of the AD, AD will increase. Assuming the economy has spare capacity, the excess AD at the original GPL creates a shortage of goods and services produced, causing an unplanned fall in inventories.

6. This will create an upward pressure on prices, and prompt profit maximising firms to increase production, leading to increased derived DD for labour and thus rising incomes.

7. Referring to the diagram below, the rise in income starting from P_1 further induces an increase in consumption, resulting in further expansion of output and hence a multiplied increase in real GDP via the multiplier process. AD increases from AD_1 to AD_2 via many rounds of induced spending. This is because one person's spending is another's income. Hence, the fiscal policy can kickstart multiple rounds of spending and income generation leading to a multiplied increase in the real GDP.

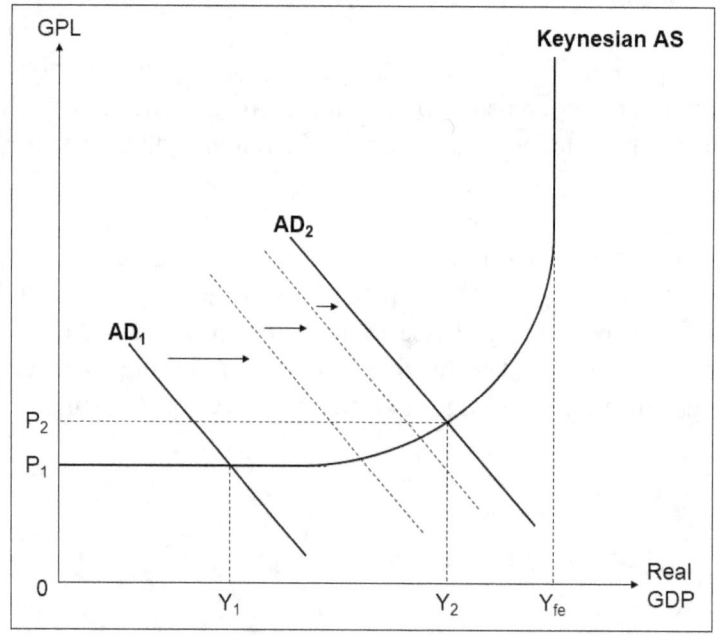

8. The economy reaches new equilibrium with a higher real GDP, at Y_2. Therefore, Expansionary FP is effective in achieving EG.

9. Through expansionary FP, there is also a greater assurance of increasing AD compared to other policies such as expansionary monetary policies. Even with a reduction in interest rates, consumption and investments might not increase due to the lack of confidence in the economy. However, expansionary FP is able to guarantee an increase in AD through direct government expenditure, such as on infrastructure. (Increased transfer payments from the government might not guarantee increases in AD — consumers could simply choose to save these transfer payments rather than spending them.)

Anti Thesis 1: Countries with small multiplier size

1. However, FP would be less effective in achieving EG if there is a small multiplier (k) value.

2. One example of this is Singapore, which has a small k value due to societal characteristics and the nature of the economy.

3. As a nation lacking in natural resources and having a prudent Asian culture as well as a compulsory savings programme, Singapore has a high Marginal Propensity to Import (MPM) and Marginal Propensity to Save (MPS). Given that k is 1/(MPM+MPS+MPT), this results in Singapore having a low k value.

4. As seen in the figure below, a country with a small k value will see a few small rounds of increased induced spending (due to large leakage), causing relatively small overall increase in AD from AD_1 to AD_2. Thus, the increase in real GDP is only from Y_1 to Y_2.

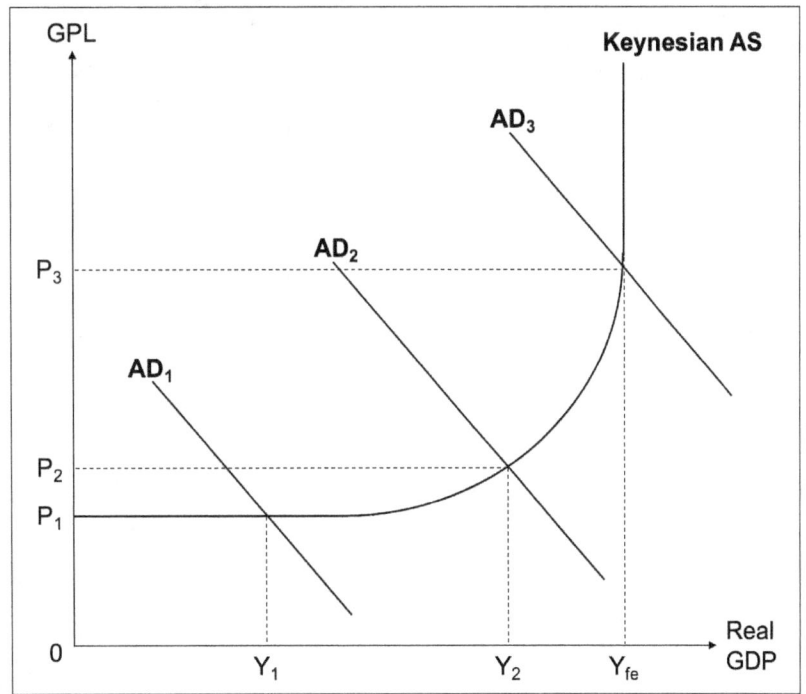

5.   However, when compared to a nation with a large k value, despite both economies beginning at the same point (Y_1), more rounds of increased induced spending and real GDP are triggered, causing an increase in AD and real GDP by a much larger magnitude than a country with small k value. The increase in AD is significantly greater (from AD_1 to AD_3), causing national income to rise greatly from Y_1 to Y_{fe}.

Anti Thesis 2: State of Economy

1.   When implementing FP, the state of the economy also has to be considered. Assuming the economy is operating near full capacity, expansionary FP could potentially trigger demand-pull inflation with limited effect on boosting EG. This is because EG cannot go beyond Y_{fe} unless there is an increase in the long-run part of the AS.

2.   Inflation would trigger uncertainty in an economy which lowers the level of investment and hence economic growth. Therefore, FP might not be a good policy in achieving economic growth, unless it can boost potential economic growth through the increase in the long-run part of AS.

3.   For example, if the government increases spending on building more infrastructure, it could be seen as an increase in quantity of capital. Hence, the long-run part of AS will increase, reducing inflationary pressures.

4.   As seen in the diagram below, with an increase in the long-run part of the AS, real GDP has increased from Y_1 to Y_2, and the increase in GPL (from P1 to P3) is relatively smaller due to the expansion of AS.

5.   However, the increase in long-run part of AS likely requires a few years. Hence, this would mean that potential growth and sustained actual growth can only be achieved after some time.

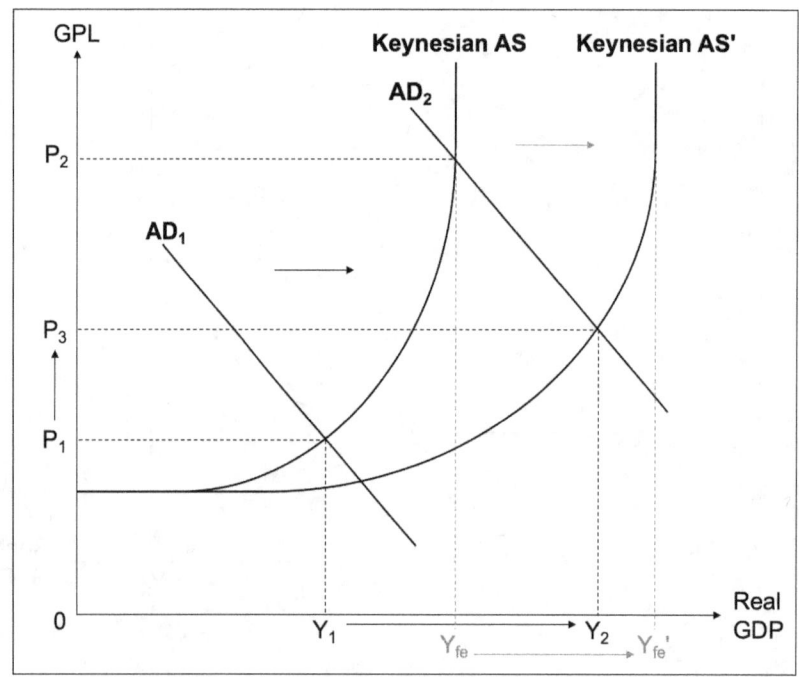

Anti Thesis 3: Crowding Out Effect

1. Additionally, the usage of such policies might induce a crowding out effect, thus limiting actual economic growth.

2. When enacting expansionary fiscal policy, if the government has limited funds to finance a budget deficit, they would have to borrow and compete with firms for loanable funds.

3. This drives interest rates up and increases the cost of borrowing, making fewer investment projects profitable, leading to a decrease in I. Thus the increased government spending is said to have crowded out private spending.

4. Therefore, overall, I may decrease, dampening the increase in AD. and rendering the fiscal policy less effective.

Anti Thesis 4: Nature of Economy

1. The effectiveness of an expansionary FP would also depend on the nature of the economy.

2. Small and open economies like Hong Kong are highly dependent on exports for EG due to limited domestic demand. Hence, an expansionary FP may have limited effectiveness in boosting EG.

Concluding Section

1. In conclusion, whether FP is effective in achieving EG depends on the state and nature of the economy, the ability of the government to increase expenditure and the size of the multiplier.

2. Due to its problems and limitations, monetary policies and supply-side policies are usually also implemented in combination with FP. Supply-side policies can target potential EG whilst expansionary monetary policies can help to reduce the crowding out effect and strain on the government's budget.

13. Evaluate the effectiveness of interventionist supply-side policies to achieve economic growth. (15)

Introduction

1. Supply-side Policies (SSPs) are policies that attempt to increase the aggregate supply.

2. The basic idea behind interventionist SSPs is that the free market economy cannot by itself achieve the desired outcome in terms of sufficiently increasing productivity and potential output and thus government intervention is required.

3. Economic growth (EG) refers to an increase in the Real Gross Domestic Product (RGDP) produced by an economy over time.

4. Economic growth can refer to actual growth or potential growth.

5. Potential growth refers to the increase in the amount of output that could be produced if all resources are fully employed. This can happen through an increase in the quantity, quality and mobility of factors of production (FOP).

6. On the other hand, actual growth refers to the annual percentage increase in the RGDP of an economy.

Thesis: How interventionist SSP can achieve EG

1. Business spending on R&D and government spending on infrastructure could help to increase the potential output of the economy. In this regard, governments enact policies that create incentives for businesses to carry out R&D, as firms would not take into account the positive externalities generated, and therefore, if left to the free market, there would be under-allocation of resources to R&D.

2. For example, Singapore's Economic Development Board offers a 30% co-funding subsidy for R&D projects related to science and technology, through its Research Incentive Scheme for Companies (RISC).

3. With advancements in technology, more output can be produced with the same amount of resources and hence an increase in the LRAS and potential economic growth occurs.

4. With the increase in productivity, unit cost of production will likely fall, leading to an increase in the SRAS as well.

5. As the general price levels fall from P to P', expenditure on domestically produced goods is spurred on, allowing the country to enjoy an increase in actual output from Y_{fe} to Y_{fe}' as seen in the following diagram.

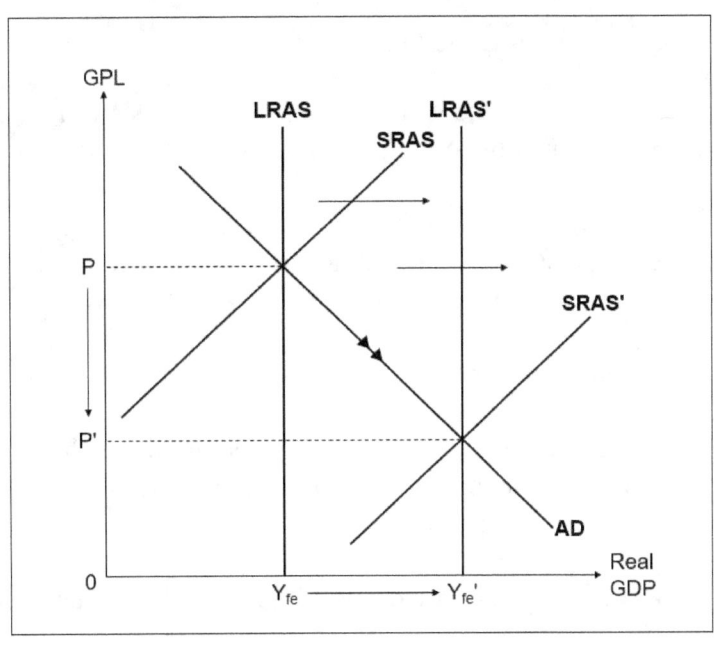

6. Moreover, interventionist SSPs could increase AD (ie. SSPs may have DD-side effects), and thus further promote actual growth.

7. For example, large-scale infrastructure projects involving road extensions involve increased government expenditure (G), a component of AD.

8. Additionally, R&D can also improve the quality of products, making them more appealing to locals and foreigners alike. This causes export revenue (X) to increase and import expenditure (M) to decrease, as there is a switch to domestically produced goods and services, thereby increasing net exports, a component of AD.

9. Referring to the diagram below, this is represented by a rightward shift of AD from AD to AD', causing an upward pressure on prices from P to P'. The increased prices incentivise firms to increase their output from Y to Y'.

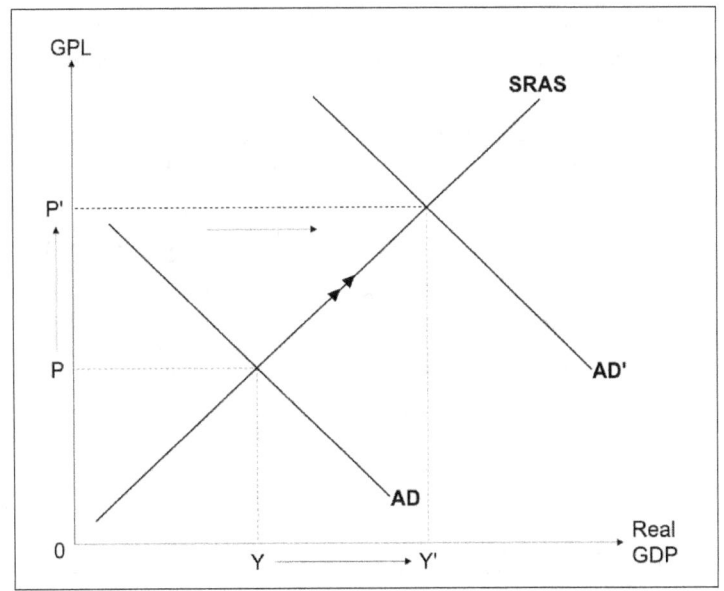

Anti-Thesis 1: Crowds out private spending

1. The ability of the government to engage in interventionist SSPs (in particular infrastructure projects) may be limited by its budget.

2. In order to finance the SSP, assuming the government lacks reserves, it would seek to loan from the public, resulting in a decrease in supply of loanable funds and an increase in interest rates.

3. This increase in interest rates increases the cost of borrowing for households and firms.

4. With the increased cost of borrowing, consumers would be disincentivised from taking loans to finance consumer expenditure, possibly causing a decrease in C, especially of big-ticket items.

5. Additionally, fewer investment projects will be profitable, thereby decreasing I.

6. Thus, a decrease in AD may result in the short-term, limiting the effectiveness of SSP in promoting actual economic growth.

7. Additionally, the decreased investment by private firms also reduced potential economic growth as fewer capitals goods are added to the economy.

Anti-Thesis 2: Long time lags

1. Interventionist SSPs in particular have significant time lags, both in the time needed to implement the policies, as well as the time taken before the policy has an impact.

2. Government policies like infrastructure projects involve large expenditures, and thus have to be approved by the legislative branch of the government. Debate on such policies could take a long time, leading to a long time lag before the policy is even implemented.

3. Infrastructure projects also take a long time to be completed. The process of building highways, roads, railways, factories and others, takes a few years at minimum. Hence there will be some time before the policy achieves an increase in productive capacity.

4. The fact that infrastructure projects are carried out over a long time period, means that government expenditure on such projects involve small, periodic injections, rather than a one lump sum stimulus. Therefore, any increases in government expenditure due to these projects might have a negligible effect on increasing AD, resulting in limited actual growth.

Anti-Thesis 3: Outcomes are uncertain

1. For one, interventionist SSPs could have highly uncertain outcomes on the supply-side of the economy.

2. Government incentives to promote R&D are highly indirect. Few companies, if any, could take on the government's offer for R&D subsidies due to the typically high R&D costs, and the amount of R&D carried out by businesses could remain stagnant in spite of the policy. Even if more R&D is carried out, there is no guarantee that the research will produce any meaningful results that allow for increased productivity. Therefore, this policy may not bring about potential and actual growth.

Concluding Section

1. Interventionist SSPs should be relied upon as a long-term measure to achieve potential growth in the economy. A wide range of such policies such as including subsidies for training and education, and tax incentives to increase investments would be crucial in ensuring that the economy continues to achieve potential and actual economic growth.

2. However, due to its limitations, interventionist SSPs are fundamentally unsuited for situations where rapid, short-term growth is required. For example, these policies would be highly ineffective and unsuitable to combat a recession. In such situations, demand management policies, namely fiscal and monetary policy, would be more suitable.

14. "Market-oriented supply-side policies will always be more effective in promoting economic growth than demand-side policies." To what extent do you agree with this statement? (15)

Introduction

1. Market-oriented supply-side policies refer, broadly, to government policies designed to influence the level of Aggregate Supply (AS) by reducing intervention and increasing competition within the economy.

2. Demand-side policies include both Fiscal and Monetary Policy.

3. Fiscal Policy (FP) refers to the government deliberately manipulating the level of taxation and government expenditure to influence Aggregate Demand (AD).

4. Monetary Policy (MP) refers to the central bank manipulating money supply and interest rates to influence the level of AD.

5. Economic growth refers to an increase in the Real Gross Domestic Product (RGDP) produced by an economy over time.

6. Economic growth can refer to actual growth or potential growth.

7. Potential growth can happen through the expansion of the amount of output that could be produced if all resources are fully employed. Hence, the productive capacity of the economy could be expanded due to an increase in the quantity or quality of factors of production (FOP).

8. On the other hand, actual growth refers to the annual percentage increase in the RGDP of an economy.

Brief Explanation of Policies

1. Market-oriented supply-side policies work by reducing costs of production and increasing the quantity and quality of factors of production (FOPs). This leads to increases in Short-Run AS (SRAS) and Long-Run AS (LRAS) which drives economic growth.

2. On the other hand, expansionary FP involves reducing direct taxes (income and corporate tax) and increasing government expenditure. Reduced income tax allows households to have more disposable income, increasing consumption (C), a component of AD. Reduced corporate tax increases the after-tax profits of firms, making more investment projects profitable, increasing investment (I). The increases in C and I work alongside increased government expenditure (G), leading to increases in AD which allow for economic growth.

3. Expansionary Monetary Policy similarly aims to increase AD. This is accomplished through central banks increasing the supply of money in the economy, which consequently decreases interest rates. Decreased interest rates reduce the cost of borrowing by consumers to finance big-ticket purchases, increasing C. Decreased interest rates also serve to increase the expected rate of return to investment projects, incentivising firms to invest, increasing I.

4. Referring to the diagram below the increases in C and I lead to an increase in AD from AD_1 to AD_2. As a result, real GDP increases from Y_1 to Y_2, signifying actual growth.

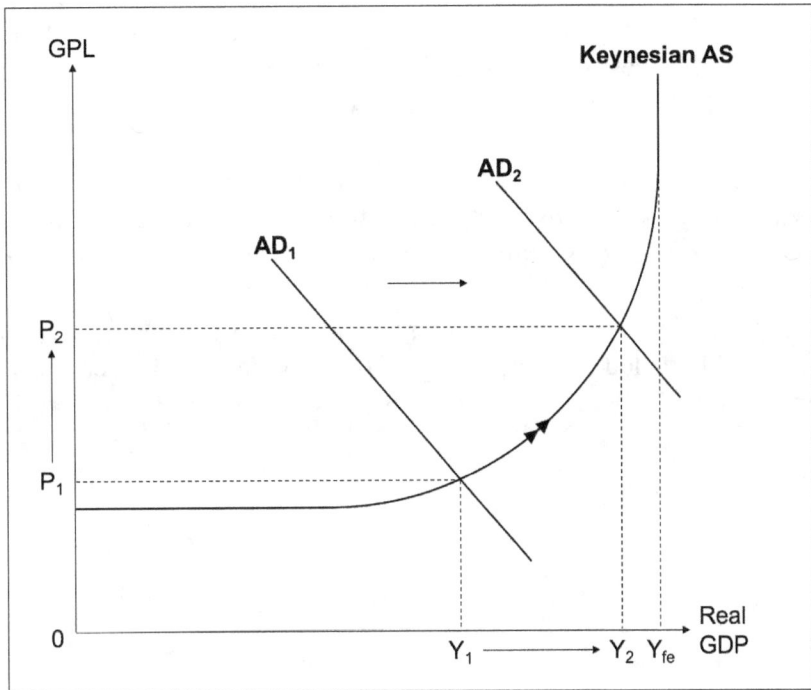

Thesis: Market-Oriented Supply-Side Policies are more effective

1. Market-oriented supply-side policies are effective in combating supply-side causes of weak EG.

2. Rising costs of factor inputs, like imported materials or labour may be the result of excessive government intervention (in the form of tariffs or minimum wages). Therefore, it would be wise for the government to tackle these root causes head on through market-oriented supply-side policies, which stand to be more effective.

3. Moreover, by removing minimum wage, reducing power of Trade Unions, privatisation and deregulation, an increase in I would be encouraged, leading to increased AD and hence boosting EG.

4. This is unlike demand-side policies, which mainly target AD, and would thus be less suitable in this case. Without dealing with the problems raised above, policies to reduce corporate taxes and lower interest rates may also be ineffective to spur I.

5. Additionally, market-oriented supply-side policies promote increased competition and efficiency, avoiding problems of government failure. Policies such as privatisation and deregulation spur productive efficiency, which in the long term is beneficial for the economy and helps to drive growth.

6. For example, during the 1970s, in the United States, there were heavy regulations placed upon banks involving interest rates and the lending/borrowing of funds. Today, with the deregulation of the banking industry, ceilings on interest rates and deposits have been removed and the industry is more competitive.

7. Also, market-oriented supply-side policies increases the productive capacity of the economy through investments which increases the quantity or quantity of capital goods, allowing for a more efficient utilisation of existing resources.

8. This is especially important when an economy is 'overheating' or facing too high levels of AD with supply-side constraints. In such cases, market-oriented supply-side policies are crucial in allowing for sustained economic growth to take place in the future.

9. Referring to the diagram below, an increase in AD from AD_1 to AD_2 while AS remained constant would have led to overheating of the economy. However, with an increase in the AS from AS to AS', RGDP can continue to increase while inflationary pressures are relieved.

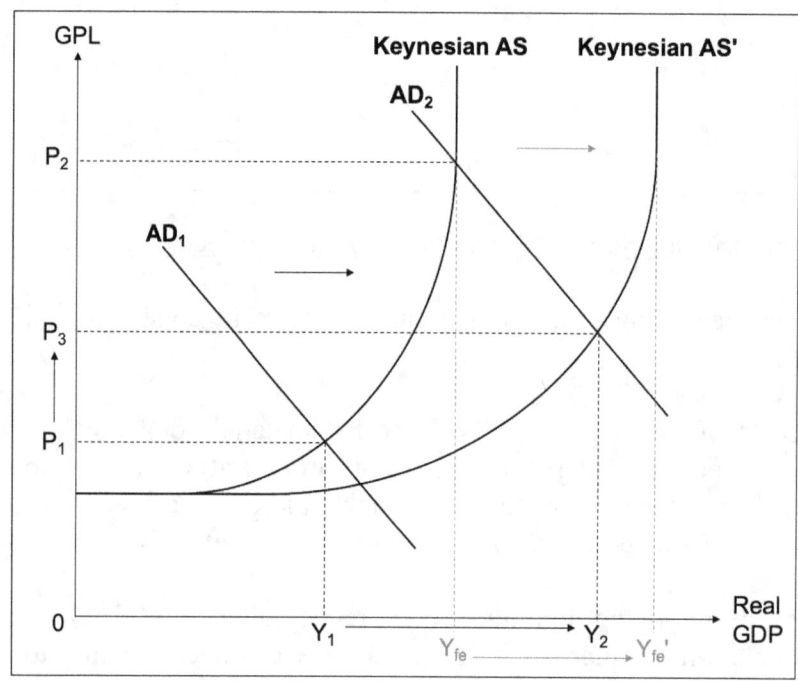

Anti-Thesis: Demand-Side Policies are more effective

1. For one, certain market-oriented supply-side policies tend to be politically unpopular, and thus many governments are hesitant to implement them. Labour market reforms, in particular, face a large amount of opposition from the working class. As a result, such policies might not be implemented to a full extent, causing them to be ineffective. For example, the UK government's plan to reduce unemployment benefits drew widespread opposition and protests from many on the streets.

2. On the other hand, expansionary demand-side policies generally do not evoke such opposition from the populace; a decrease in taxes (under fiscal policy) would be a welcome measure by many. Therefore demand-side policies can be implemented more aggressively and thus more effective at promoting growth.

3. Additionally, due to resistance from Labour Unions, etc, some market-oriented supply-side policies can take quite a long time to implement.

4. This is unlike Monetary Policy, which can be unilaterally implemented by the Central Bank, and thus can be quickly put into place.

5. Market-oriented supply-side policies may also have uncertain outcomes. Unlike fiscal policy, where there is a direct and certain effect on AD through increased government expenditure, supply-side policies may not be as effective in ensuring an increase in spending and output.

6. There is also an additional benefit from demand-side policies through the multiplier effect where one person's spending is another's income, leading to multiple rounds of spending and income generation. Through the successive rounds of increase in AD leading to real GDP increasing, the increase in RGDP is greater than the initial increase in G.

Concluding Section

1. Market-oriented supply-side policies are not always more effective than demand-side policies.

2. For one, demand-side policies might be most effective in promoting economic growth during a recession – monetary policy can be implemented immediately during the onset of a recession with fiscal policy as a direct and aggressive measure of increasing AD through an increase in G.

3. Market-oriented supply-side policies are more effective as a long-term solution to increase productivity and competition while promoting a conducive environment for I and thus EG, rather than a short-term solution to reverse a recession.

15. To what extent can supply-side policies help in fighting inflation? (15)

Introduction

1. Demand-side policies refer to deliberate government attempts to influence the level of Aggregate Demand (AD) in the economy, to achieve various macroeconomic goals.

2. Supply-side policies (SSP) refer to deliberate government attempts to influence the quantity, quality and mobility of Factors of Production (FOPs), thereby affecting the level of Aggregate Supply (AS) in the economy to achieve various goals.

3. In this case, to fight inflation, the government may seek to implement contractionary demand-side policies, or supply-side policies, to reduce the level of inflation.

Thesis: Supply-Side Policies are more effective

1. Supply-side policies involve a wide variety of possible measures aimed at increasing the quantity or quality of FOPs. One possible measure involves subsidies for training and education schemes targeting workers. These subsidies incentivise workers to undergo training and upgrade their skills, increasing the quality of labour. This allows existing labour force to be more productive, expanding the productive capacity of the economy, seen as an outward shift of the Keynesian AS curve.

2. For example, the Singapore government has in place the SkillsFuture initiative which provides a rebate of S$500 for workers to attend various skills training courses.

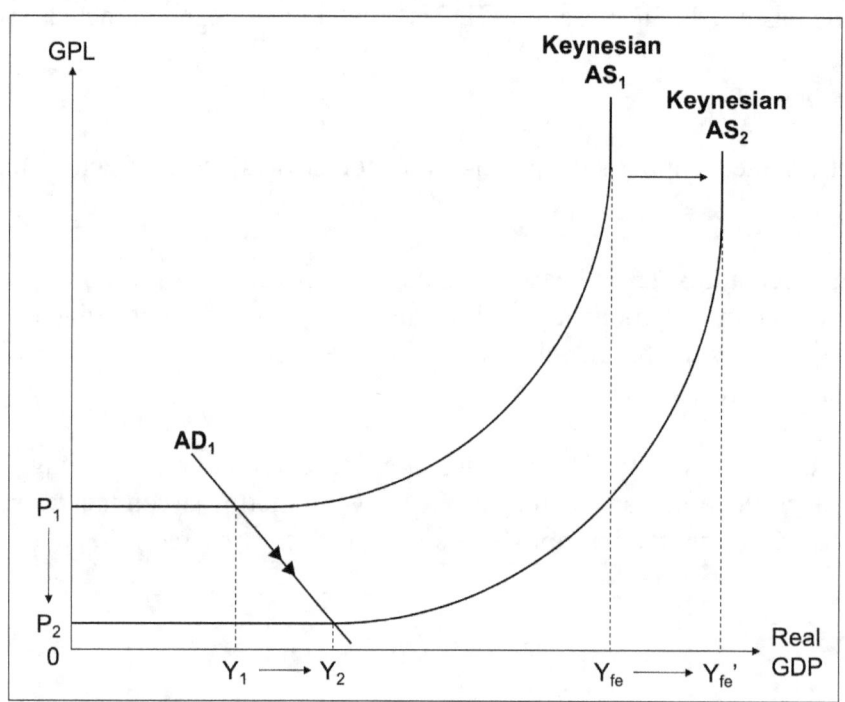

3. Referring to the diagram on the previous page, with the upgrading of workers, the Keynesian AS has increased from AS_1 to AS_2 with the productive capacity expanded. Assuming the economy was initially undergoing inflation at P_1, the decrease in GPL to P_2 would help to curb inflation.

4. SSPs would be the most suitable option to deal with cost-push inflation, as it effectively targets the root causes of the inflation, thereby being more direct and effective. To tackle cost-push inflation, it will be more of Market Oriented SSP in terms of the reduction of Trade Unions' power to curb wage push inflation. Also, short-run SSP could include subsidies given to firms. For example, the Indian government subsidises fuel so as to increase the SRAS.

5. Also, SSPs are effective in dealing with demand-pull inflation, where AD is increasing when economy is operating at or near full capacity. Referring to the diagram below, as AD increases from AD_1 to AD_2, there is a large initial increase in GPL from P_1 to P_2 which denotes demand-pull inflation. However, with an increase in the long-run part of AS and hence spare capacity, demand-pull inflation is moderated and the increase in price is only from P_1 to P_3.

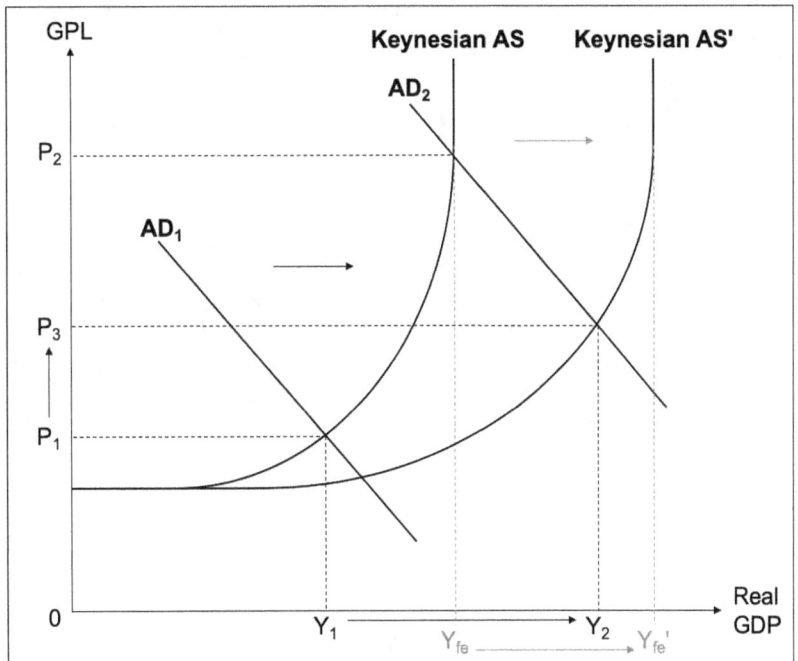

6. Furthermore, SSPs have less severe repercussions on the economy than demand-side policies do. Said demand-side policies, which target inflation by reducing the level of AD in the economy, could possibly stunt economic growth rates or even plunge the economy into a recession (should the extent of the reduction in AD be severe enough). On the contrary, since SSPs target potential growth, there is no such risk of a slowdown in growth occurring.

Anti-Thesis: Demand-Side Policies are more effective

1. Contractionary demand-side policies involve monetary policy (MP) or fiscal policy (FP). In this case, the MP would involve raising interest rates, increasing the cost of borrowing to finance investments or big-ticket consumer purchases, leading to reduced consumer and investment expenditure.

2. Similarly, the FP would involve increasing taxes, which deter consumer and investment spending, and decreasing government expenditure. This leads to a decrease in the Consumption (C), Investment (I) and Government expenditure (G), all components of AD, thereby causing AD to fall. Referring to the diagram below, AD falls from AD to AD', while GPL falls from P to P'.

3. For example, in light of the strong economic recovery the US has faced since the 2008 Great Recession, the Federal Reserve has steadily raised benchmark interest rates to stave off inflation. From 2016 to 2018, the interest rate was gradually raised from 0.25% to 2.5% over 9 increments.

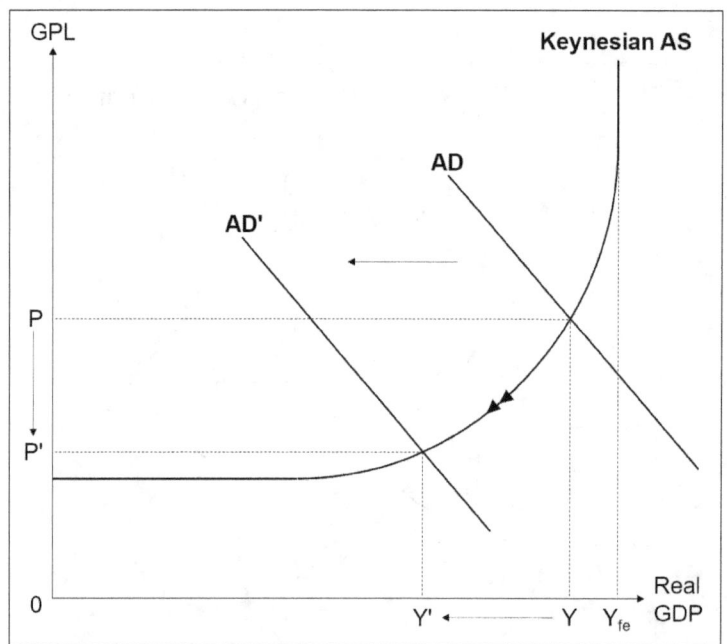

4. Demand-side policies could be more effective than SSPs as they involve a shorter time lag. For example, monetary policy can be quickly implemented, since interest rates can be unilaterally decided upon by the central bank, without requiring lengthy bureaucratic procedures.

5. On the other hand, supply-side policies (such as the aforementioned subsidies for training and education) need to pass through the government and be debated and approved before implementation, a process that can take months, in which time inflation could already be spiralling out of control.

6. Also, there are huge policy drawbacks of SSPs, namely that the government might take months or even years to gain sufficient support to enact the policy (especially controversial ones, for example those targeting Trade Unions). Even after being enacted, there is a risk of the policy not succeeding. For example, the French government has faced a large difficulty in garnering the public's support for its policies with Macron's popularity declining.

7. Additionally, some demand-side policies are able to curb inflation without placing a strain on the government's budget. For example, raising interest rates does not require any monetary expenditure on the government's part, whereas supply-side policies do. Therefore, monetary policy is more effective as the central bank can go all in without worries of debt or funding issues.

8. Furthermore, demand-side policies have more certain outcomes. For example, contractionary Fiscal Policy involving a decrease in government expenditure, a component of AD, will have a very certain outcome in decreasing AD. Whereas the success and outcomes of supply-side policies depend on many factors out of the government's control – for instance, training subsidies are only effective if workers are receptive to the training and learn from it.

9. For example, in Singapore's case, the government has long been aggressively implementing training and education programmes, but missed its productivity growth target for many years, reflecting that the effectiveness of such supply-side policies is highly uncertain.

Concluding Section

1. Ultimately, the effectiveness of either policy does depend on the root causes of inflation. If the inflation is due to cost-push factors, then supply-side policies could be most effective in dealing with these factors directly. Likewise, if the inflation is due to demand-pull factors, then contractionary demand-side policies should be used.

2. The severity of the inflation also needs to be considered. If the inflation rate is high, or increasing, the government should consider demand-side policies as they tend to have more immediate and certain outcomes.

3. Ideally, a combination of both demand- and supply-side policies is needed. Supply-side policies are a long-term solution that prevents future inflationary pressures and allows the economy to grow whilst avoiding or fighting inflation.

16. "The rate of inflation can be most effectively reduced through the use of monetary policy." To what extent do you agree with this statement? (15)

<u>Introduction</u>

1. The inflation rate measures the percentage change in the general price levels within an economy over time. '

2. Changes in the inflation rate could be influenced by demand-pull and/or cost-push factors.

3. Demand-pull inflation is caused by excessive aggregate demand (AD) within the economy, whereas cost-push inflation is caused by increases in the cost of production experienced by firms.

<u>Explanation of Monetary Policy</u>

1. Contractionary monetary policy refers to deliberate attempts by the central bank to reduce the supply of money within the economy, so as to increase interest rates. Interest rates refer to the cost of borrowing or the rate of returns on savings.

2. The increase in interest rates will increase the cost of borrowing by households to finance big-ticket purchases, thereby disincentivising households from consuming, causing a decrease in consumer expenditure (C), a component of Aggregate Demand (AD). Simultaneously, the increase in interest rates also increases the cost of borrowing to firms, thereby reducing the expected rate of returns to investment projects, making fewer investment projects profitable, thereby causing investment expenditure (I) to fall.

3. The decrease in C and I consequently leads to a decrease in AD. The fall in AD creates a surplus of goods in the economy at the original general price level (GPL), thereby placing a downward pressure on the price levels, hence curbing inflation.

4. For example, to curb overheating in the economy and a soaring inflation rate that was approaching double digits, the People's Bank of China began to raise interest rates incrementally from 2004 to 2008. In total, the interest rate was increased from 5.31 % to 7.47 %.

<u>Thesis: Monetary Policy is the best</u>

1. For one, monetary policy can be fine-tuned by the central bank in order to suit the magnitude of the problem. This allows for nuanced adjustments to be made to aggregate demand, in order to bring the inflation rate down to desired levels, thereby allowing for it to be especially effective. This ability to fine-tune the economy is not evident in other economic policies considered.

2. Furthermore, monetary policy is arguably the quickest policy that can be implemented. Since decisions about money supply and interest rates can be unilaterally made by the central bank, without lengthy bureaucratic procedures or government approval, a contractionary monetary policy can be quickly put in place to curtail a soaring inflation rate. With other policies that have long time lags, inflation may have long spiralled out of control by the time the policy gains governmental approval and is enacted.

3. Additionally, monetary policy also does not have any negative impacts on the government budget. This is opposed to policies like supply-side policies, which often place a strain on the government's budget, and therefore cause governments to be hesitant in implementing them to the fullest extent. With monetary policy, there are no such worries or constraints.

Anti-Thesis 1: Monetary Policy doesn't work

1. For one, the outcomes of monetary policy are highly uncertain. Should there be an excessively optimistic business outlook in the economy, households may continue to consume, and firms continue to invest, regardless of interest rate hikes. This could render the policy ineffective to deal with inflation.

Anti-Thesis 2: Fiscal Policy is better

1. Contractionary fiscal policy involves the government raising direct taxes (income and corporate tax) and decreasing government expenditure (G). Increased income taxes reduces the disposable income available to households, deterring consumption. Increased corporate taxes reduce the after-tax profits of firms and hence also reduce the expected rate of returns to investments, making fewer investment projects profitable, thereby deterring investment. The decreases in C, I and G lead to a decreased AD, which lowers inflation.

2. Unlike monetary policy, fiscal policy has more certain outcomes. The decreased government expenditure, for one, will have a more definite effect in curtailing aggregate demand. Therefore, this enables fiscal policy to be able to deal with severe inflation in a more effective manner than monetary policy.

Anti-Thesis 3: Supply-side policies are better

1. Monetary policy is only able to directly and effectively curtail demand-pull inflation. It would be ineffective to combat cost-push inflation as it is unable to deal with the root causes of the problem.

2. In such cases of cost-push inflation, supply-side policies can more effectively deal with the issue.

3. For example, during the OPEC oil embargo that was enforced upon the US in the 1970s, the cost of oil rose exponentially, in turn driving up the costs of production for all firms. This translated to increased prices borne by consumers alongside decreases in production activities and real output.

4. In such cases, supply-side policies such as abolishing the minimum wage, subsidies, removal of tariffs on imported inputs all serve to reduce the cost of factor inputs and thus the unit cost of production.

5. On the other hand, using contractionary monetary policy to curb cost-push inflation would be ineffective in dealing with the root causes, and would result in severe repercussions to the wider economy in the form of increased recessionary pressures.

Concluding Section

1. Monetary policy is not necessarily the best policy to curb inflation.

2. Monetary policy is best used to deal with moderate levels of demand-pull inflation, and to fine-tune inflation rates back to target levels.

3. Ultimately, there are varied causes of inflation and the policies each have their own strengths and weaknesses. A multi-pronged approach would be best as each policy can cover up the flaw of the other policy. For example, policies such as fiscal policies are suitable for use in the short-run to curb inflation while supply-side policies to expand the productive capacity of the economy can be used in the long-run. And monetary policy could be used as a final adjustment to allow the economy to precisely attain target levels of inflation. Hence, there is each a policy meant for both the short and long-run, working together to reduce the rate of inflation.

17. Discuss the view that the best way to reduce unemployment is through the use of demand-side policies. (15)

Introduction

1. Unemployment refers to the number of individuals who are of working age, able to work, but are without work and actively seeking a job.

2. Unemployment in an economy comprises the Natural Rate of Unemployment (NRU), which refers to any unemployment present when an economy is producing at its full-employment output level, as well as demand-deficient unemployment, which is unemployment resulting from a lack of Aggregate Demand (AD).

3. There are three further types of unemployment that comprise the NRU – frictional, seasonal and structural.

4. Frictional unemployment refers to unemployment as a result of being between jobs, or fresh entrants to the labour force looking for a job.

5. Seasonal unemployment occurs when the demand for a particular skill changes on a seasonal basis due to variations in needs.

6. Structural unemployment occurs when there is a mismatch between the skill-sets offered by those who are unemployed, and the skills that are currently in demand by firms/ employers. It can also be due to labour market rigidities and geographical immobility of workers.

Explanation of demand-side policies

1. Demand-side policies refer, broadly, to government policies designed to influence the level of Aggregate Demand (AD).

2. Expansionary Fiscal Policy refers to the government reducing direct taxes (income and corporate tax) and increasing government expenditure (G). The decrease in income tax serves to increase the disposable income available to households, incentivising them to consume more, thereby increasing consumption (C). The decrease in corporate tax increases the after-tax profits of firms, thereby making more investment projects profitable, increasing investments (I). These increases in C, I and G work to increase AD.

3. Expansionary Monetary Policy refers to the Central Bank intervening to increase the supply of money, thereby lowering interest rates. Decreased interest rates reduce the cost of borrowing by households to finance big-ticket purchases, thereby incentivising greater consumption, increasing C. Decreased interest rates also decreases the cost of borrowing for firms, and as a result, more investment projects are profitable, increasing I. The increases in C and I thereby increase AD.

<u>Thesis: DD-side policies are the best way</u>

1. For one, demand-side policies are highly effective in combating demand-deficient unemployment, which is the result of firms laying off workers when real output and production activities decline. Demand-side policies are able to target the root cause of demand-deficient unemployment, namely the weak AD in the economy, and therefore constitute the best and most suitable policy to target demand-deficient unemployment.

2. Referring to the diagram below, an initial rise in AD starting from AD_1 would lead to an unplanned rundown of inventories by firms. Profit maximising firms increase production, thus increasing their derived demand for factors of production, including labour. Hence, employment increases and demand-deficient unemployment hence decreases. The increased income causes a round of increased induced consumption, which triggers another round of increased production which will lead to a further increase in income and induced consumption (multiplier effect). Overall, the AD has risen from AD_1 to AD_5, with the dotted lines representing each round of the multiplier effect.

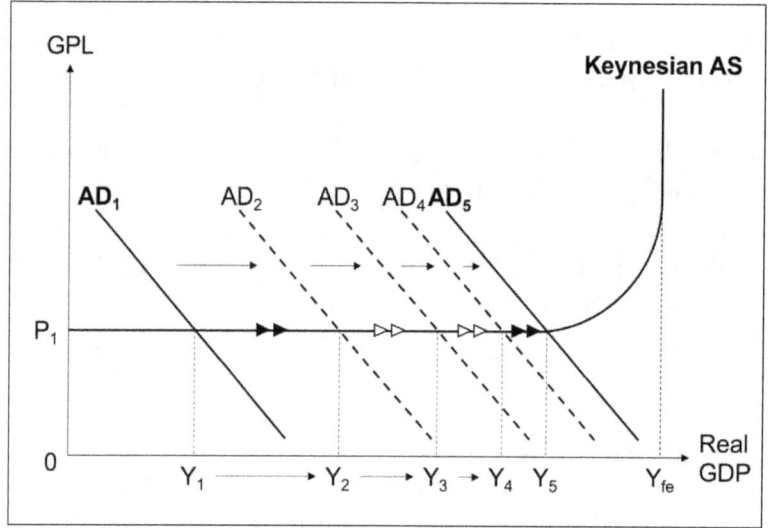

3. Short-run supply-side policies (SSP) are able to increase RGDP but would lack the exponential growth afforded by the multiplier effect, since these SSPs work mostly through increasing the SR part of the AS curve.

4. Furthermore, monetary policies can be fine-tuned to allow for nuanced adjustments that suit the magnitude of the problem. For example, in the onset of the 2009 Great Recession, the US Federal Reserve was able to gradually decrease its interest rates over several months, to fine-tune economic performance and to judge the severity of the problem.

5. Demand-side policies generally have a shorter time lag than supply-side policies, which thus allow them to be more effective at reducing unemployment. Monetary Policy has a very short implementation time lag, since money supply and interest rates can be unilaterally decided by the central bank, without requiring lengthy bureaucratic government approval.

6. Fiscal Policy, through the increases in government expenditure allow for a direct and concrete means to increase Aggregate Demand and thus the demand for workers. This is in contrast to supply-side policies, which not only take a long time to implement, but also have uncertain and indirect effects on unemployment, such as R&D policies. R&D typically takes a long time to be completed, and there are very uncertain outcomes on its success. Even if R&D is successful, there might be a displacement of workers by technology which will instead increase unemployment.

Anti-Thesis: SS-side policies are more effective

1. Fundamentally, demand-side policies are unable to deal with unemployment existing at full-employment output level. Since demand-side policies work only to increase AD and real output, once the economy is already operating at full-employment, demand-side policies thus become redundant and ineffective at tackling any further unemployment.

2. SSPs can reduce unemployment in a non-inflationary way where the growth in AD is accompanied by a corresponding growth in AS. For example, through the policies which will be explained below, there will be an increase in the quality and quantity of labour, allowing for an expansion of the economy's productive capacity. This is reflected as an increase in both the short-run and long-run part of the AS curve, where AS increases from AS_1 to AS_2. Even with an increase of AD_1 to AD_2, the GPL remains constant at P_1 where demand-pull inflation is removed.

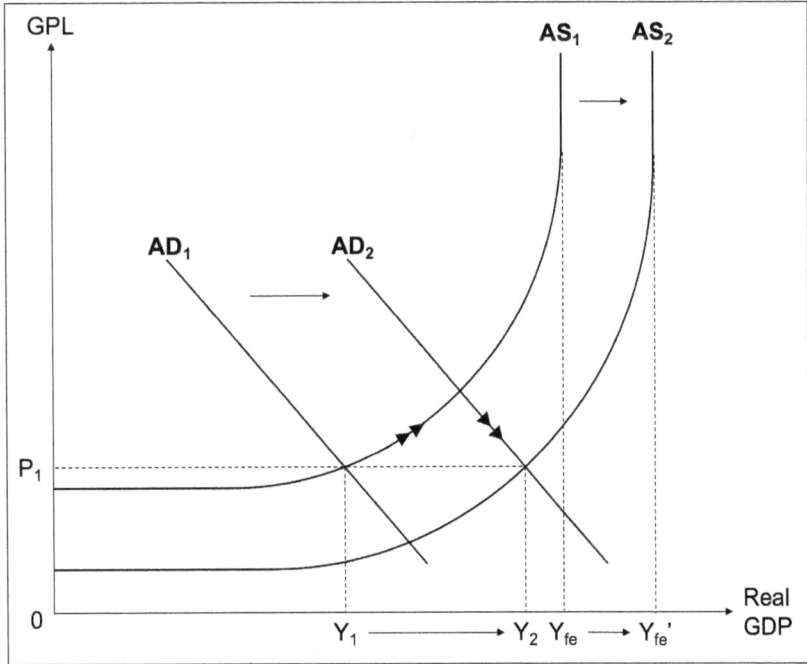

3. Firstly, SSPs are very effective in reducing structural unemployment. For example, the Singapore government has in place its SkillsFuture initiative, which provides S$500 in rebates for all Singaporeans to attend vocational training programmes. This is important to allow those who are structurally unemployed to upgrade their skills to better suit those which employers are currently demanding. Hence, this policy effectively tackles structural unemployment.

4. Furthermore, the encouragement of skills training can help to reduce seasonal unemployment. With a wider range of skills, workers can still be gainfully employed during the "off seasons".

5. Secondly, SSPs are also able to effectively reduce frictional unemployment. One case-in-point relates to the Singapore government's latest initiative, the MyCareersFuture scheme, which provides an online platform for job-seekers to search for job vacancies across a multitude of industries. This allows the unemployed to have better access to information relating to job vacancies, thereby facilitating the process of finding a suitable job, and in the process reducing frictional unemployment.

Concluding Section

1. Ultimately, much depends on the type of unemployment concerned. For demand-deficient unemployment, demand-side policies are, without a doubt, the best solution.

2. On the other hand, for unemployment which exists at full-employment output level, supply-side policies are the only solution possible.

3. As various causes of unemployment can exist in the economy at any point in time, the best approach would be to implement a combination of policies. In this way, unemployment can probably be reduced both immediately and also avoided in the future.

18. "Fiscal policy is the most effective way of bringing an economy out of recession." To what extent is this statement valid? (15)

Introduction

1. An economy is said to be in a recession if it suffers a consecutive decline in actual output for a period of 2 months. A recession could be caused by demand-side or supply-side reasons.

2. Expansionary Fiscal Policy (FP) refers to the government deliberately increasing government spending (G) and/or reducing direct taxes (T) in an attempt to spur spending, thereby increasing AD and real GDP.

Explanation and Example

1. For example, during the 2008 Great Recession, American's real GDP faced a consecutive decline from 2007 Q4 to 2009 Q2.

2. As a result, the government implemented a series of public works projects to build infrastructure such as roads, and in doing so increasing government expenditure (G) by a total of US$ 105.3 billion.

3. Personal income taxes were reduced, thereby increasing the disposable income available to households, and stimulating consumer spending, increasing consumer expenditure (C).

4. Corporate taxes were also reduced, to increase firms' after-tax profits, increasing the rate of returns to investment projects, making more investment projects profitable, thereby increasing investment expenditure (I).

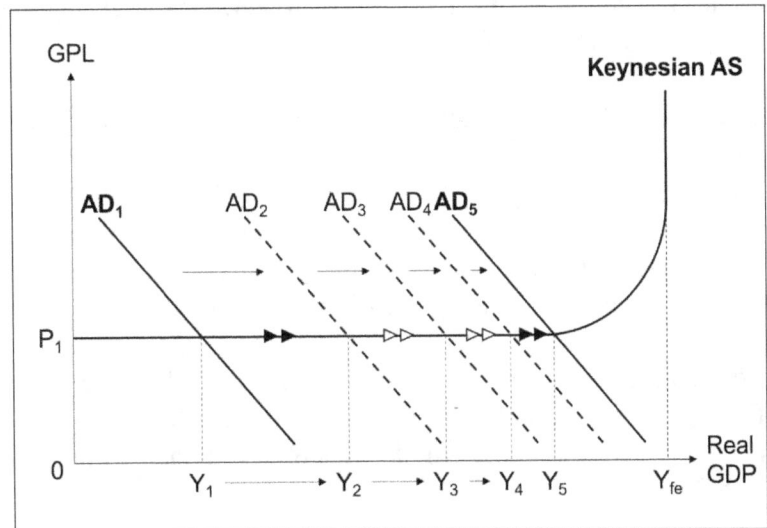

7. Referring to the diagram on the previous page, an initial rise in AD starting from AD_1 would lead to an unplanned rundown of inventories by firms. Profit maximising firms increase production, thus increasing their derived demand for factors of production, including labour.

8. The increased income causes a round of increased induced consumption, which triggers another round of increased production which will lead to a further increase in income and induced consumption (multiplier effect). Overall, the AD has risen from AD_1 to AD_5, with the dotted lines representing each round of the multiplier effect.

5. Hence, the increase in AD from AD_1 to AD_5 would increase real output from Y_1 to Y_5 while general price levels remain at P_1, assuming the economy is operating at the Keynesian range.

Thesis: Fiscal Policy is most effective

1. For one, Fiscal Policy is most effective as it has a direct effect on Aggregate Demand. Increasing government expenditure has a direct and sizeable impact on increasing spending, allowing for greater certainty and effectiveness of the policy to boost AD.

2. Additionally, Fiscal Policy is also aggressive enough to be able to pull the economy out of a deep recession. The combined effect of direct government spending and tax cuts makes Fiscal Policy a more effective solution, as the FP influences more components of the AD as compared to other policies like Monetary Policy.

Anti-Thesis 1: Fiscal Policy is less effective

1. For one, Fiscal Policy is subject to major time lags. It takes a long time for the government to debate and finalise proposals on what to increase G on and where to cut taxes. Also, the spending might not be immediate, as the government might spend over a few years if it engages in an infrastructural project. Hence, a recession could very well worsen severely in the meantime.

2. Additionally, should the government need to borrow money to finance the Fiscal Policy, this could lead to the crowding out effect. The government borrowing loanable funds leads to a decrease in the supply of loanable funds, which consequently causes interest rates to rise. The rise in interest rates makes it more expensive for consumers to borrow money to purchase big-ticket items, and for firms to invest. As a result, this could decrease C and I, potentially causing the FP to be ineffective at increasing AD.

3. Referring to the diagram on the next page, the FP should theoretically increase AD from AD_1 to AD_3. However, due to the crowding out effect, the increase in AD is damped and AD ends up at AD_2, which renders the FP less effective than what it could have been.

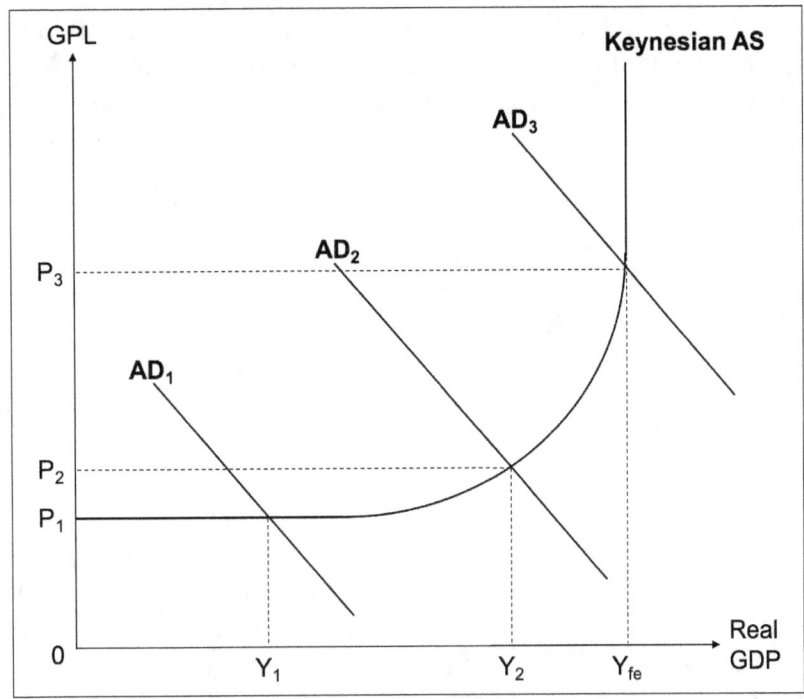

4. Furthermore, fiscal policy is unable to tackle the root causes if there are supply-side causes to the recession. For example, Fiscal Policy would be ineffective in combating a recession due to rising oil prices, as occurred in the US in 1973 due to the OPEC oil embargo. This is because the Fiscal Policy is unable to fundamentally target the root of the issue.

5. The effectiveness of the FP is also dependent on the nature of the economy. For small and open economies such as Hong Kong and Singapore which are export-dependent, FP is likely to have a weaker effect as compared to larger economies like the United States.

Anti-Thesis 2: Monetary Policy might be better

1. Consequently, other policies might be more suitable to help the government tackle a recession.

2. Monetary Policy involves the Central Bank increasing the supply of money in the economy, thereby lowering interest rates. The lowered interest rates make it cheaper for consumers to borrow money to purchase big-ticket items, and causes more investment projects to be profitable. Therefore, this increases C and I, increasing AD and real GDP.

3. Since Monetary Policy can be unilaterally decided upon by the Central Bank without any bureaucratic procedures, it can be quickly implemented at the start of a recession. Furthermore, as it does not require any expenditure on the government's part, there is no risk of a crowding out effect.

4. However, the outcomes of a Monetary Policy are highly uncertain, as an excessively pessimistic business outlook could deter any increases to C and I. Furthermore, there is a possibility of a liquidity trap where interest rates are low while saving rates are high. This would cause MP to be ineffective where customers avoid bonds and prefer to save their money while awaiting higher interest rates and for bond prices to fall.

Anti-Thesis 3: Supply-Side Policy might be better

1. Supply-Side Policies involve policies aimed at improving the quantity, quality and mobility of Factors of Production (FOPs). For example, market-oriented supply-side policies could be considered – deregulation of key industries or labour market reforms are aimed at increasing productivity, which would lead to an increase in Aggregate Supply and RGDP.

2. With an increase in the quantity and quality of FOPs, Keynesian AS increases from AS_1 to AS_2 and the productive capacity of the economy increases. With investors' confidence in the economy increasing due to a highly skilled workforce, I increases and hence AD rises from AD_1 to AD_2. With an increase of both AD and AS, real GDP increases from Y_1 to Y_2, bringing the economy out of recession.

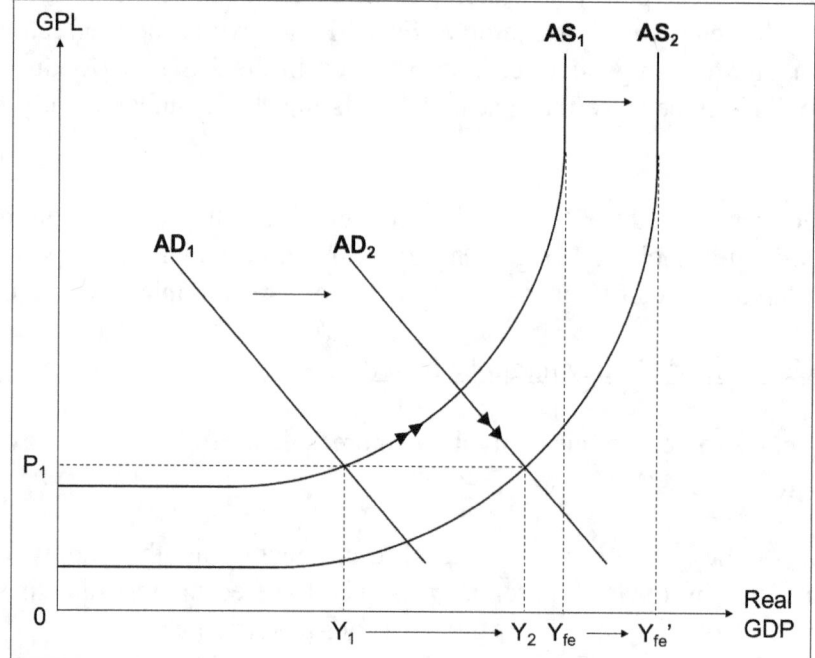

3. These supply-side policies have the potential to be more effective, as they may be able to better target root causes of the recession such as the lack of economic competition that has deterred investments and lowered confidence.

4. However, like Fiscal Policy, they involve time lags to implement and to take effect. A lot of careful studies, and even campaigning have to be put in place to ensure that the deregulation and labour market reform policies will really be suitable and well-mapped as there are typically many trade-offs involved in such policies.

5. Furthermore, the outcomes of a Supply-Side Policy are also highly uncertain, and the benefits to economic growth might not be significant. For example, deregulation might not increase investments due to a lack of confidence in the economy.

Concluding Section

1. In conclusion, Fiscal Policy has mixed effectiveness during a recession due to its time lags and the possibility of a crowding out effect.

2. A more effective solution would be to use Fiscal and Monetary Policy simultaneously. The Monetary Policy, which is quick to be implemented, can help to prevent the budding recession from worsening and also avoid the crowding out effect by reducing interest rates.

3. Supply-Side Policies can also be the most effective solution if the recession is due to supply-side constraints.

4. A combination of policies would be most ideal as each policy has its own strength and weakness. During the 2009 recession, Singapore adopted a multi-pronged approach where she adopted a combination of expansionary FP, MP (currency depreciation), coupled with short-run SSPs (wage subsidies). These policies complemented each other well.

19. "An increase in aggregate demand may not lead to an increase in real national income." To what extent is this statement valid? (15)

<u>Introduction</u>

1. The central economic problem of scarcity holds that there are limited resources available while there are unlimited wants of man.

2. Consequently, it is not surprising that there will come a point where the economy is simply unable to produce more, when all existing scarce resources are already fully utilised.

<u>Thesis 1: Increase in AD causes increase in real national income</u>

1. Keynesian theory states that an increase in AD would increase the real national income if the economy was operating below full-employment output level.

2. For example, during the 2008 Great Recession, the US economy faced negative growth rates, as AD weakened due to an excessively pessimistic business outlook. The economy was most likely to have been operating along the horizontal segment of the Keynesian AS curve – where there is a lot of spare capacity.

3. The US government's 2009 stimulus package had led to an increase in AD and hence real national income through large amounts of government spending on infrastructure projects and increased availability of credit.

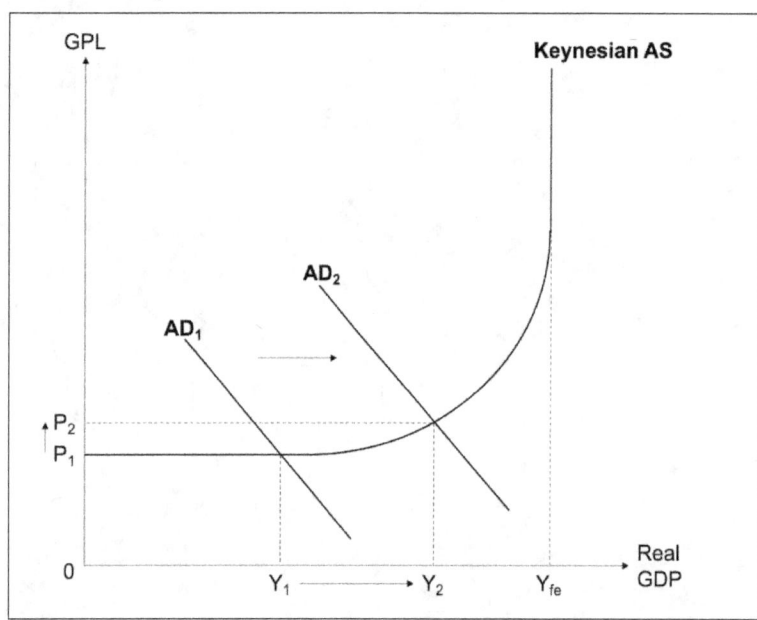

4. Referring to the diagram below, as Aggregate Demand increases from AD₁ to AD₂, the idle resources in the economy would have been used to increase production, allowing for real output and national income to have increased. Similarly, as resources are being used and becoming scarcer, factor prices are bid up, leading to a subsequent increase in the General Price Levels (GPL) from P_1 to P_2.

Anti-Thesis 1: Increase in AD may not increase real output

1. However, according to Keynesian theory, should an economy already be operating at full-employment output level Y_{fe}, any increases in AD would only serve to increase GPL and not real output. This is because Keynesian theory holds that an economy cannot produce beyond Y_{fe}.

2. For example, during the Lawson Boom of the late 1980s, the UK economy experienced a period of rapid growth owing to high consumer and investment expenditure. This period of economic boom was characterised by soaring double-digit inflation rates – an indication that the UK economy was 'overheating' or producing at the full-employment output level.

3. Under this scenario, as consumer and investment expenditure continued to grow, the economy was unable to experience much increase in real output. This is because all available resources in the economy were already being fully utilised.

4. Referring to the diagram below, as AD continued to increase from AD₁ to AD₂, real output remained at the full-employment level Y_{fe}, with soaring inflation that saw GPL increase significantly from P_1 to P_2.

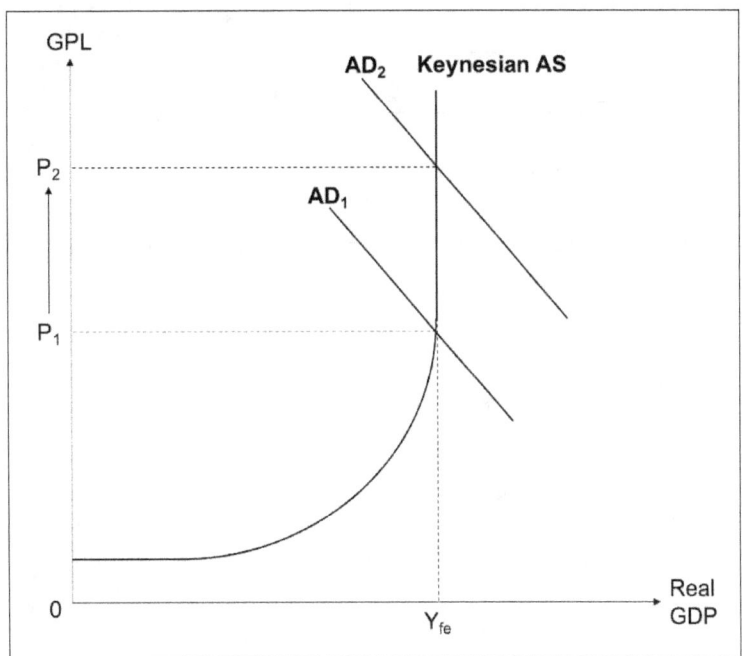

Thesis 2: Real national income can still increase, beyond Y_{fe}

1. Alternatively, according to a neoclassical perspective, increases in AD will always allow for increases in real output. This is true even if the economy is operating at full-employment output level.

2. Using the above example of the UK economy during the Lawson Boom, the increases in AD would have allowed real output to increase beyond Y_{fe}. Neoclassical theory holds this to be possible, as existing factors of production can be over-exerted to produce more – for example, forcing workers to work overtime, and having machines and factories operate through the night.

3. In the short-run, this would have allowed the increase in Aggregate Demand from AD_1 to AD_2 to see real output increase from Y_{fe} to Y_1.

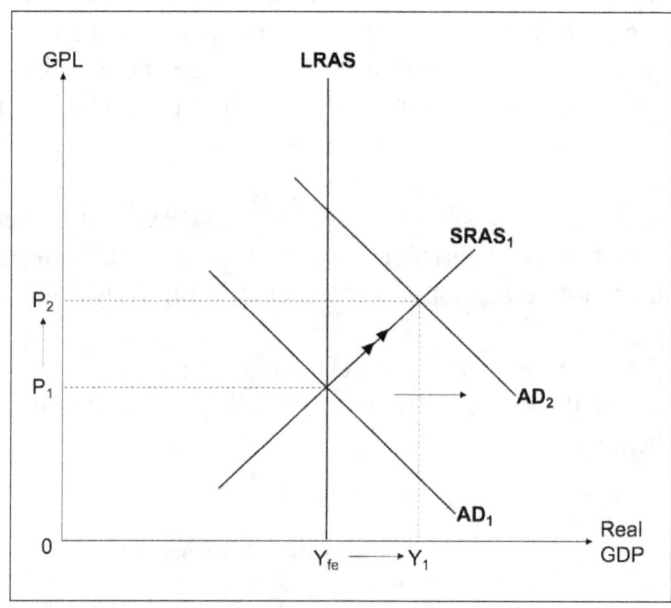

Anti-Thesis 2: It cannot increase in the long-run

1. However, neoclassical theory holds that this increase in real output cannot be sustained in the long-run.

2. In the long-run, when factor prices become flexible, the market will self-correct to eliminate the inflationary gap previously created. The economy will always return to the full-employment output level in the long-run.

3. In this case, by forcing workers to work overtime in order to produce more output, in the long-run, workers will begin to demand for increased hourly wages to compensate for loss of leisure and additional wages to maintain real wages due to higher inflation rates. Firms will also be bidding up wages in order to obtain more workers to sustain the higher production levels. These increased wages would increase the labour costs. Therefore, this causes a decrease in the Short-Run Aggregate Supply from $SRAS_1$ to $SRAS_2$, which reduces real output, bringing the economy back to Y_{fe}.

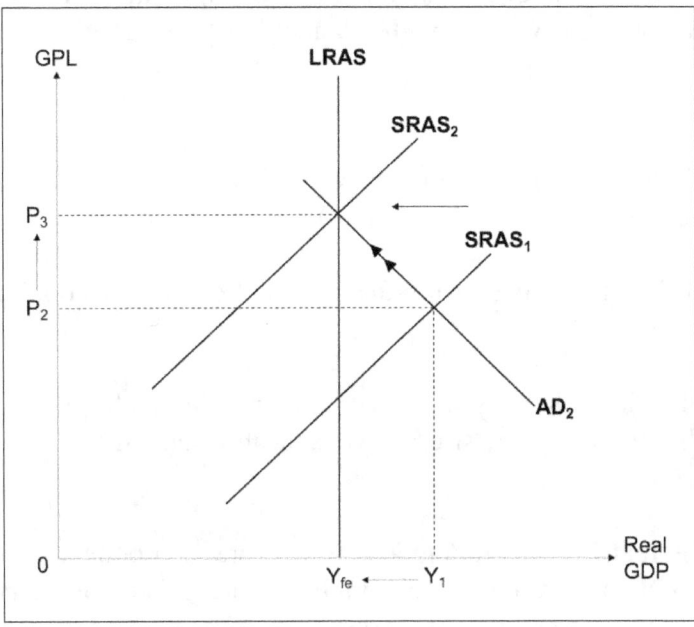

Concluding Section

1. In conclusion, the statement is definitely true – increases in AD may not lead to an increase in real national income.

2. This occurs when the economy is producing at full-employment level according to Keynesian theory, or when viewing the economy in the long-run according to neoclassical theory.

20. Evaluate the view that the benefits of economic growth will always outweigh the costs. (15)

Introduction

1. The effects of economic growth (EG) can be considered based on its impact on other macroeconomic indicators, such as inflation, unemployment, income distribution and the balance of payments, as well as on the standard of living.

Benefits: Higher SOL

1. Standard of living (SOL) refers to the economic and social wellbeing of the residents in a country and consists of material and non-material aspects.

2. Material well-being consists of the quantity and quality of goods and services available for consumption.

3. Non-material well-being consists of the less tangible, quality of life factors including the quality of the environment, stress levels, health standards and the amount of leisure available.

4. An increase in real GDP, assuming at a higher rate than population growth, would lead to higher real GDP per capita, which implies more goods and services available to the average citizen. Unemployment should also be decreasing as demand for labour increases. Thus, material SOL increases.

5. This might also improve non-material SOL as the increase in incomes would allow for greater peace of mind, with less stress about fulfilling necessities. The higher incomes would also allow for more consumption of education and healthcare, literacy rates and health standards.

6. In addition, the increase in real GDP would lead to income tax revenue. When workers use their increased earnings on consumer goods, the government can also collect increased consumption tax revenue as well. The increased in production also suggests that more workers may be employed and the government will have to spend less on welfare benefits – food stamps, unemployment benefits, etc.

7. Thus, the Government would have increased funds to spend on a host of other programmes to improve SOL – income redistribution through stronger welfare, greater provision of merit goods (like healthcare) and so on.

Cost 1: Reduce SOL

1. However, an increase in real GDP per capita reveals little about who actually gains the added income in the economy.

2. For example, although New Zealand enjoys robust economic growth, the standard of living of lower-income households has not improved. This is due to stagnating real wages, combined with decreasing welfare benefits that leave the poor with even less financial support than before. The economic growth has mainly benefitted the upper-class in New Zealand, who are enjoying higher real wages and a decreased tax on high-income earners. Income tax evasion also remains rampant among the rich, allowing them to avoid paying their fair share of taxes. Rising house prices also disproportionately benefit the rich, who are homeowners, at the expense of the poor, who are renters and thus now have to bear higher rent costs.

3. Furthermore, as production may generate negative externalities, such as through disposal of chemical waste into rivers, this could lead to highly detrimental effects (in this case, health problems caused by pollution) on third-parties (those living near the affected area) who are not directly involved in producing or consuming the good(s) involved. The negative health effects of pollution would lead to a reduction in non-material SOL.

4. It is also pertinent to note the extent of growth. Should growth in an economy be too rapid, it could be an indication that existing factors of production are being exploited in an unsustainable manner. Sustainable economic growth refers to growth that is able to meet the needs of the present generation without compromising the ability of the future generations to meet their own needs. For example, Indonesia's economy has been growing rapidly, owing in part to the fishing industry, which accounts for 3% of the country's real GDP. However, overfishing is rampant and is gradually depleting fish stock, compromising the ability of fishermen in the future to continue fishing. In this vein, Indonesia's rapid growth comes at the expense of future growth.

Cost 2: Structural Unemployment and Inequity

1. Economic growth driven by technological advancements imply that certain skills would become obsolete, with demand for such skills falling, correspondingly resulting in structural unemployment.

2. For example, McDonald's has been shifting to using machines for front-end services. Customers can now order using large touchscreens, negating the need for workers to operate cash registers. This may result in structural unemployment for those retrenched. These are likely to be low-skilled workers with few marketable skills, and would be hard off finding employment elsewhere where other skill-sets are demanded (e.g. engineers, IT, biomedicine).

3. Therefore, this segment of the population will be unable to enjoy the benefits of economic growth, and suffer income losses instead. This concern is especially pertinent now with the rise of Artificial Intelligence, which threatens to pose a disruptive force across many industries, potentially rendering millions of jobs obsolete.

4. This further worsens income distribution. The upper-class will benefit from increased incomes as they are the ones with higher education levels and skills that are less replaceable by technology, while the lowly paid low-skilled workers face joblessness.

5. These issues can also occur through export-oriented economic growth. Different industries face different prospects with some growing and some declining in the face of foreign competition. Thus, demand for skills change and those retrenched may not have the right skills to switch to the growth industries. For example, when cheaply-produced Chinese textiles flooded the Greek market, local textile producers were unable to compete with the cheaper foreign substitutes. Many Greeks lost their jobs, resulting in high levels of structural unemployment.

Cost 3: DD-pull inflation

1. Demand-pull inflation presents a problem should it be significantly high. This occurs when Aggregate Demand (AD) is increasing in excess of Aggregate Supply (AS), driving prices higher as resources are used up and become increasingly scarce.

2. EG can be accompanied by demand-pull inflation as reflected in the diagram below, where persistent increases in AD cause the economy to operate near or at full-employment output level, resulting in high levels of demand-pull inflation.

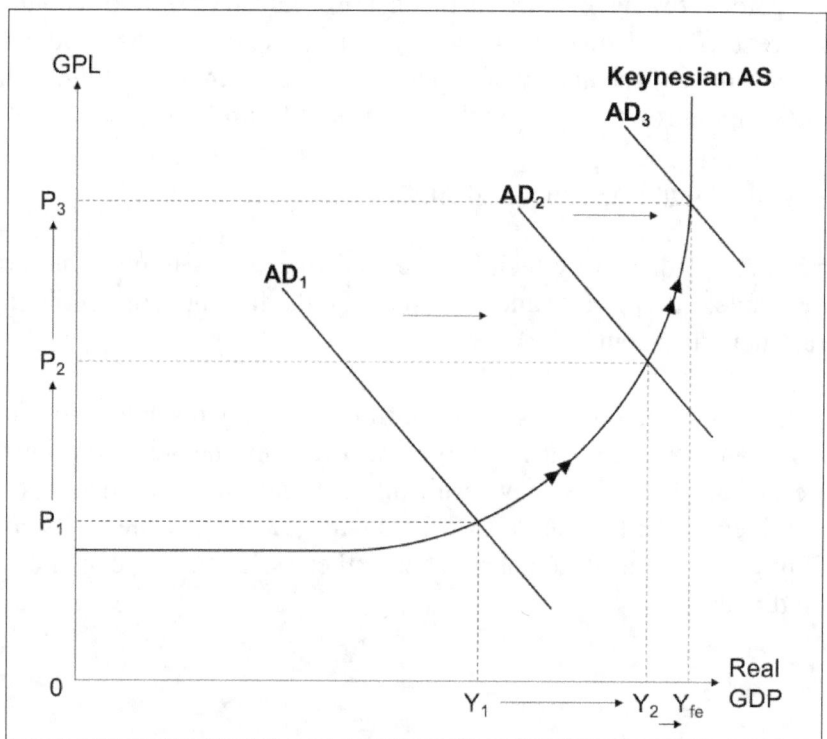

3. From the previous diagram, GPL rises from P_1 to P_2 and subsequently P_3. Demand-pull inflation could worsen the standard of living of fixed-wage earners who will see the real value of their wages falling. Fixed-wage earners refer to salaried employees receiving a set dollar figure per hour of work. Should nominal incomes of these workers increase at a slower pace than inflation, this translates to an effective decrease in their real wages; they have reduced purchasing power, thereby enjoying fewer consumer goods and services, causing their material SOL to drop.

4. This is likely to cause further increases in income inequity – low-skilled workers who tend to be less well-off are the ones whose nominal wages are stagnating and material SOL falling.

Cost 4: Worsening Current Account (CA) and Balance of Payments (BOP)

1. As economic growth leads to increases in real income per capita, the increase in GPL leads to an increase in demand for imports, hence increasing the import expenditure.

2. Consumers might also change their consumption patterns, favouring luxury goods. These luxury goods may be imported from other countries and are perceived as being of 'higher quality', as compared to cheaper locally-produced substitutes.

3. Hence, these cause the import expenditure of the country to increase, leading to a worsening balance of trade. Consequently, this could lead to deficits in the current account, hindering the achievement of a favourable BOP.

Concluding Section

1. Generally, the benefits of economic growth should outweigh the costs though it cannot be said to always be so.

2. The sources of growth, state of the economy and presence of government policies to mitigate adverse effects are key factors. With increased budget arising from economic growth, this should increase the government's ability to, for instance, pursue income redistributive policies, and supply-side policies to achieve potential economic growth and tackle structural unemployment.

3. Greater economic growth can also provide more "room" for the government to address issues of environmental and sustainability concerns, as addressing these issues may require accepting a lower rate of economic growth.